C000263975

Francis Nenik is a pseudonym; the author prefers to remain anonymous. He was born in the early 1980s and lives in Leipzig. Nenik boasts numerous publications in renowned magazines such as *Merkur*, *Edit* and *Words Without Borders*, some of which were produced for radio. His debut novel *XO* was published in the form of a loose-leaf collection. His award-winning essay 'The Marvel of Biographical Bookkeeping' (tr. Katy Derbyshire) was published by Readux Books in 2013, *Coin Operated History* (tr. Amanda DeMarco) by Fiktion in 2016.

Katy Derbyshire was born in London and has lived in Berlin for over twenty years. She is an award-winning translator of contemporary German writers, including Olga Grjasnowa, Angela Steidele and Clemens Meyer. Having taught literary translation in New York, New Delhi and Norwich, she now co-hosts a monthly translation lab and the bi-monthly Dead Ladies Show in Berlin. Katy is the publisher of the V&Q Books imprint.

Journey through a Tragicomic Century
The Absurd Life of Hasso Grabner
by Francis Nenik

V&Q Books, Berlin 2020
An imprint of Verlag Voland & Quist GmbH
First published in this form in Germany as *Reise durch ein tragikomisches Jahrhundert* in 2018 by Verlag Voland & Quist GmbH

Editing: Florian Duijsens
Copy editing: John Owen
Cover design: Pingundpong*Gestaltungsbüro
Typesetting: Fred Uhde
Printing and binding: PBtisk, Příbram, Czech Republic

www.vq-books.eu

Journey through a Tragicomic Century

The Absurd Life of Hasso Grabner

Francis Nenik

Translated from the German by Katy Derbyshire

What a life story.
It is both astounding and regrettable that it has never been documented, but perhaps also understandable at a time seething with hurriedly written memoirs which barely tell us about history and hardly tell a story.

Daniel Flügel in the *Potsdamer Neuesten Nachrichten*,
on the centenary of Hasso Grabner's birth, 2011

Contents

Setting Out

21 October 1911 is not exactly an outlier when it comes to dates in world history. In Vienna, an archduke marries a princess, and the local emperor makes an amusing toast. In Utica, New York, a gigantic Mississippi farmer and a puny travelling-circus employee empty the contents of their revolvers into the body of a lion clutching its 12-year-old girl tamer in its jaws, and in Leipzig, a boy is born by the name of Hasso, who would later claim not to know the slightest thing about his father.

A mother, of course, is present in the case of young Hasso, as is right and proper, and the father is to emerge later on, albeit from a heap of files. And why not? The men in the family have an obsession with paper, after all; the boy's great-uncle even wrote the second volume of Marx's *Capital.*

That is, he didn't write it exactly, more transcribed it, which is no mean feat either, when you consider that Marx, on his death, left not a finished book but a manuscript so hieroglyphic that his companion Friedrich Engels needed not just a whole year, but also a personal secretary to get the papers Marx bequeathed him – 'barely grouped, let alone processed' – even approaching print ready.

That very secretary, it turns out, was the great-uncle of the little boy who has just been born here, on this page, and while the one is called Hasso Grabner, the other is called Oscar Eisengarten. Incidentally, that name, garden of iron, is one of those benevolent contradictions that only the 19th century could produce.

In any case, when the publisher Otto Meissner ran the presses at Leipzig's Reusche printing plant in July 1885, it was Eisengarten's transcription of *Capital* that served as the source.

A quarter of a century later, little more is left of the great-uncle than a small gravestone weathered by English rain, and all that young Hasso has left is a mother who earns a meagre living as a salesgirl and a christening certificate that reveals to him that his father was not only unknown but also unmarried to his mother, for which reason the pastor felt obliged to prefix 'extra' to the pre-printed word 'marital' on the certificate.

In short, the family has seen better days and money is tight, even with his grandmother and aunt supporting his mother, so at the age of 12 Hasso Grabner is sent away to the nearby town of Halle and then on to various foster families in Gera, where he perhaps finds a roof for his head, if not a home. What the boy does not manage, however, is to complete school. By the time he returns to Leipzig in 1926, just turned 15, his mother is on her deathbed.

Politically, though, Hasso Grabner is almost an old hand by this point. Not only is his family – at least as far as their memory serves – part of the original lineage of Saxon social democracy, oh no. Hasso Grabner himself has also done something for the revolution already, stealing ammunition at the age of 12 and 'spying' on the despised *Jungstahlhelm* junior paramilitaries, so it comes as no surprise that, in a narrative résumé composed for the Socialist Unity Party's* regional directorate 45 years later, he declares outright that he 'took part in the Armed Struggles of 1918 to 1923 as far as my childish capabilities allowed.'

Memory, as every child knows, is the basis of history. Ideology, however – as will become clear later on – is the form in which history is expressed.

In 1926, though, the Socialist Unity Party does not yet exist, and Hasso Grabner's progression in life does not yet require safeguarding in writing. History will have to seek some other medium; though no one would imagine it to be a magazine about psychic powers.

Admittedly, the *Zentralblatt für Okkultismus* is not exactly what the common or garden social democrat keeps on their bedside table, and the communists with their striving for scientific precision generally give a wide berth to the *Monatsschrift zur Erforschung der gesamten Geheimwissenschaften*. Hasso Grabner, however, spends day after day with the aforementioned Central Journal of Occultism and the Monthly Periodical on Research in the Entire Esoteric Sciences. He has to: Max Altmann's publishing house, where Grabner has found work as a gopher, has made it its purpose to bless humankind with spiritualist literature by the ton. And indeed, Leipzig's eager readers practically begin baying for the extrasensory, and since the police have lifted the ban on the fiddle-faddle of fortune-telling, business has been all the better.

And so it transpires that Hasso Grabner, the bespectacled young communist with his neatly parted hair, provides local marketgoers with articles on telepathic plants, recruits admirers for the miraculous Brazilian medium Mirabelli even among university professors, and in the process also learns about seeing humans as antennae, after which he receives pages and pages of clairvoyants' impressions on the future of Germany – just as his own future is gradually ticking away, attempting to tiptoe past him unnoticed.

Essentially, Fräulein Future has already made it out of the door by the time an unpredicted event occurs in Max Altmann's publishing house on Leipzig's Frommannstrasse, on 23 May 1928. On that day, just before five thirty in the afternoon, an elderly gentleman enters the building and asks to speak to Max Altmann in person. He does not state a reason for his request, but it appears so urgent that he is let through. When the gentleman arrives at the publisher's desk he introduces himself as an envoy of the Association of German Booksellers and asks, still slightly out of breath after running the 800 metres from Platostrasse to Altmann's villa, whether the good publisher might suggest someone to be trained at the German Booksellers' Academy. The starting date, however, is soon, in essence that very day, hence the urgency and the rather improper perspiration...

Max Altmann thinks it over, mentally going through all his junior staff. Then he says no.

In the next room, Hasso Grabner has been eavesdropping. There's no time to think it over, that much he knows. So he opens the door in front of him, enters the publisher's office – and suggests himself as a trainee.

The gentleman from the Association has no idea that the 16-year-old lad standing before him hasn't even finished school. And Max Altmann consents, for better or worse. Twenty years ago, he published a paper on clairaudience, and it would appear that Hasso Grabner has just come across it in the next room.

Two years later, in April 1930, Hasso Grabner passes his apprenticeship with flying colours, the best in his year. His prize: a trip to Brazil to gain work experience with a German-speaking bookseller in Blumenau. But Hasso Grabner turns it down. A convinced leftist, he is afraid of missing the revolution in Germany. Aside from which, the miraculous medium Mirabelli has already told all there is to be told in Brazil, *foretold* it even, and had it relayed and confirmed via the Central Journal through the Leipzig philosophy professor Hans Driesch:

I would like to mention another very impressive phenomenon: a door 'closed' itself at a distance of circa five metres from the medium. The light was always good, in some cases very bright.

4. VIII 1928

Signed: Professor Hans Driesch

No One Knows Any More

It is 14 September 1930. The world is in the midst of a great depression, the Weimar Republic in the midst of a Reichstag election, and Hasso Grabner still hasn't experienced a revolution. Instead, there is unemployment, a rise in votes for the National Socialists, and no sign of improvement on the horizon. These are, if you like, shitty times, and even the miraculous medium Mirabelli is at a loss: 'A chair moved in such a way that the front legs were lifted, banged against the floor and then turned in a circle.'

Hasso Grabner, meanwhile, does not want to turn in circles; Hasso Grabner wants to do something. Having joined almost every leftist organisation he could get his hands on (or that could get its hands on him) over the past few years, including the Communist Youth Federation back in 1929, he became a card-carrying member of the Great Communist Party of Germany, the KPD, in August 1930. And because merely being a communist on paper is not enough for him, he gets himself sent to Berlin to the KPD's Rosa Luxemburg Central Party School, where he is taught the theoretical basics of his new political homeland. For five whole months, he attends long lectures in the school's impressive villa on Kurze Strasse, studying dialectic materialism, political economy and communist tactics. By the time he gets back to Leipzig in November 1930, it is raining – and the Dominican Order also returns to the north of the city, having departed at the Reformation in 1539.

Perhaps it's a dream or perhaps only a memory short-circuited somewhere along its route through the mind; that is, its resistance to fictions abandoned and its reality value reduced to near zero – in any case, one night it seems to Hasso Grabner as though there are a thousand young communists in Leipzig, the cradle of social democracy. And he ought to know, seeing as he has been sub-district secretary of the Communist Youth Federation since 1930 and thus familiar with the organisational work of youth recruitment. And yet that too is not enough for him: Hasso Grabner, the trained bookseller as restless as he is officially jobless, wants not just to administer communist ideas, but also to take them out of the party headquarters and into the city, into workplaces and homes and spiritually spoiled minds.

That same year, he founds a factory cell for young communists on the premises of one of Europe's largest cotton spinning mills, which soon becomes the most important communist cell in the entire city, and – at least in the eyes of its good three dozen members – has enough thread to dream of world revolution and spin a version of previous and future history all of its own.

Reality, however, looks different, and instead of mass uprisings and barricades, there are art afternoons and craft activities. The revolution needs preparing, after all. And so, Leipzig's young communists spend their weekends painting banners and pasting printed paper onto walls, organising meetings, publishing newspapers and promoting the communist cause outside the city's entertainment venues.

This is not particularly attractive and nor is it exactly profitable, and when tens of thousands do come – for instance at Easter of 1930, when the Communist Youth Federation of Germany holds its annual National Youth Meeting in Leipzig, with the local federation secretary pulling the strings in the background and the KPD chairman Ernst Thälmann* speaking in the foreground – the police spoil the communists' revolutionary fun.

A tussle breaks out among the 80,000 demonstrators at the closing rally, two police officers shoot at the crowd, kill one participant – and get lynched themselves.

What may sound like an extreme case has become political normality by this point, in Leipzig and across all the state of Saxony, and while some are crafting their version of the world revolution out of printers' ink, paint and paper, others are obtaining guns and knives, and forming combat squadrons, defence associations and protection leagues, their members all carrying sturdy canes; and those sticks weren't made for walking.

Alongside the sticks, there are shirts, assault straps, leather puttees, peaked caps and boots, because this is the deal: every outfit has its own outfit and, as always, the matching deference is a part of the dialectical package – first the uniforms draw the young men, then the young men don the uniforms.

And then? Then all that's missing is the right names. And so, at some point at the end of the Weimar Republic, the communist side has the Youth Federation people fighting alongside the Storm Falcons and the Antifascist Young Guard, the paramilitary Red Defence Squadrons, Red Youth Stormers and Red Front Fighters Alliance men, not to forget the Red Youth Front, which sounds like a mixture of the Red Youth Stormers and the Red Front Fighters Alliance, but actually has its very own shade of red, just like the proletarian combat groups and the numerous local groups named after their respective centurions.

The social democrats, in contrast, take a more traditional approach to naming, and boast the Young Socialist Workers and the tightly organised Reich Banner Black-Red-Gold, which in turn is flanked by combat squadrons that have not only telephones but complete telecommunications units with their own system of coded flashing lights, which send signals all across Leipzig and if necessary up to 40 kilometres outside the city, enabling their motorised members to take immediate action when Nazi troops like the Stahlhelm, the Frontbann or the Young German Order attempt attacks in concert with the SA and SS.

Essentially, at the end of the Weimar Republic, everyone is fighting everyone else, and the only thing capable of creating clarity seems to be violence.

Communists fight social democrats, social democrats fight national socialists, national socialists fight communists, and then back to the beginning and start all over again. Yet that is not yet nearly all. Communists sometimes also disrupt SPD events along with national socialists, social democrats join forces with communist combat groups against the Nazis, and social democrats on occasion take action with the Nazis against the KPD, who in turn never tire of attacking defectors from their own ranks. In general, especially with the communists, the defence organisations only follow the party's orders to a limited extent, so it comes as no surprise that the KPD's East Saxony leadership at some point declares the aggressive whippersnappers of the Red Front Fighters Alliance to be nothing but 'semi-idiotic syndicalists with Communist Party contribution cards in their pockets'.

And in Leipzig? The next killing soon comes along, with the local chairman of the Young Socialist Workers stabbed to death by a young communist while distributing leaflets on 15 August 1931. That puts paid to any chance of a united front between the SPD and the KPD. In the cradle of social democracy lies a dead boy of 19.

Hasso Grabner, meanwhile, keeps out of the worst battles. The favoured site of his confrontations is the city library, not the streets. Grabner reads Nietzsche, Maeterlinck, Luxemburg. He doesn't read Thälmann.

When the Saxon branch of the KPD relocates its offices from Dresden to Leipzig in 1932, Hasso Grabner is appointed to the inner leadership circle and entrusted with the 'Opponents' portfolio in the field of youth work. He, the former social democrat, is now responsible for encouraging the SPD's 'left' groupings to secede to the 'right' of the KPD. Arguments for crossing over are provided through *Sozialismus ist das Ziel*, a journal sectarian enough to build a bridge between the shores, with socialism as the destination, as the title suggests. Grabner writes the articles himself, while his girlfriend does the duplicating.

And what do you know – the plan works, and soon the first Young Socialist Workers are turning their backs on the old SPD and their fronts towards the young communists and their great party. That is just the beginning, and over the following months the number of individuals switching sides in Leipzig makes constant strides. In some districts, the group that splinters off is so large that the few remaining members have no option but to disband. There's simply no known cure for the powers of persuasion possessed by the converted, as we know from the history of political medicine.

In the KPD itself, the common belief by now is that the bourgeois world has long since ceased to flourish and is in rapidly deteriorating health, if not on its deathbed. The communists see the Weimar Republic of 1932 as deeply embroiled in a domestic crisis, with the collapse of the capitalist imperialist system imminent; the arc of history cannot possibly avoid leading straight to the dictatorship of the proletariat.

However, history ignores the principles proclaimed by the communists, takes a right turn driven by millions on 30 January 1933 and erects its own dictatorship.

In Leipzig, Hasso Grabner and his comrades know immediately for whom the bell tolls, and after thousands protest against Hitler's appointment as Reich chancellor on the evening of 30 January, the communists give up their headquarters the very next morning and go underground, united in conspiratorial groups of five. In their arms they carry leaflets, typewriters and duplicating machines.

No one is willing to use the word collapse, of course, not at this point. Instead, they are giving themselves some breathing space in full knowledge that it won't last long. History has simply lost its bearings briefly and will soon return to normal. All the more so because the direction is clear for the communists – and will remain clear while submerged underground. The KPD's hierarchical structure continues to determine its political work now that it's illegal, at any rate, and the party leadership calls on the submerged communists to keep in contact 'with the top'. At the top, however, they are picked off and arrested one by one, and as early as March 1933 Hasso Grabner detects 'an almost complete shattering of illegal operations'.

Grabner himself is working on a building site in the south of Leipzig at this point, constructing a reservoir with hundreds of other labour conscripts. But that's just the official version. Unofficially, he is the political head of an illegal party cell that commenced its work on the building site as early as February. This time too, it's not long before Grabner's group becomes the most important in the city, just like three years before in the Leipzig Cotton Mill. Reservoirs, as Hasso Grabner knows, are perfect places to submerge oneself.

And yet there is a difference, for the communists in general and for Hasso Grabner in particular, as now the laws of illegal operations apply. Grabner knows what they look like in theory. In March

1933 he learns first-hand that they're very different in practice. Over the space of a few days he receives dozens of parcels, none with a sender's address or any other possibility of returning them, and by the time he opens the final package on the evening of 6 March 1933, he knows that all the material previously hidden among Leipzig's young communists is now assembled under his roof. The vehemence of the fascist terror has washed it all up here, and the Nazis' election win on 5 March does nothing to return it. On the contrary. In the election's wake, the last inhibitions fall, doors are broken down, inhabitants and their belongings searched, and more than a thousand people are arrested in Leipzig. Yet the Nazi thugs don't discover Hasso Grabner on his revolutionary paper island. Or perhaps they don't want to discover him, perhaps they want him to play the decoy a little longer for his shipwrecked comrades. Hasso Grabner senses, at any rate, that there is a fine line between submerging and drowning.

Not only is the restless Grabner employed on the building site as a labour conscript and deployed as his cell's political secretary, he also has a third place and thus a third task: he is one of Leipzig's most important communist couriers. His headquarters are in a small tobacconist's shop in the east of the city, where he collects illegally produced leaflets, newspapers and books, and goes on to distribute them.

Three hundred metres away from the tobacconist's, at 5 Frommannstrasse, Max Altmann is publishing the last issue of his Central Journal of Occultism. It is made up of a long book review. Its title is *Streiflichter ins Dunkle* – sidelights into the dark.

And so it goes on, the year '33, and one thing's for sure: 'It's a shitty year! The stinking zenith, or rather nadir, of what have truly been enough shitty years.' The whole apparatus is smashed, and love is all over too. Hasso Grabner decides to leave his girlfriend.

If anyone knows why, it's him, if he does at all. Nonetheless, it is a thoroughly strange notion: separation. And that while all around them, one communist after another is being dragged out of hiding places, and ties are being severed everywhere. But what can he do? Hasso Grabner decides to go to his girlfriend so as to remove himself from their equation. But when he gets there she's gone. The Gestapo has already cut the tie he was meaning to sever.

When Hasso Grabner finally gets word of his girlfriend, he finds out she has been taken to prison and examined. The verdict can be summed up in one word: pregnant.

On her brief release from prison, months later, to give birth, Hasso Grabner decides to turn the separation into a ceremony. He doesn't want his son to grow up illegitimate. The two marry on 30 April 1934. Then his wife goes back behind bars. Hasso Grabner is married, separated and tied down.

What follows is summer. Long and hot and sticky. A cliché of a summer. A summer that leaves its imprint on paper. On page 53 of the almanac *Daten und Fakten zur Leipziger Stadtgeschichte*, in the column 'Annual Average in °C', the box after the year 1934 is grey. In it is a number: 11.1 degrees. The highest average temperature, to this day. Because the summer was so long and hot. The sun is said to have burned down on Leipzig for 65 days in a row. On one of those days, Hasso Grabner is arrested.

To be precise, it is 31 July, and Hasso Grabner is not the only one the Nazi henchmen drag out of the depths of a backyard bedsit and into the dazzling light of a Gestapo cellar that day. Alongside him, up against the wall, are another 30 communists, their eyes wide and white as the light, trembling and colourless and shivering with cold.

The indictment is simple, the crimes clear as day. The young communists have papered entire blocks with flyers, painted giant antifascist slogans on the roofs in red paint and filled all the city's letterboxes to the brim with illegal newspapers.

That's how we imagine it. But that's not how it is. That's not how it is at all.

It's all far smaller, far more banal – and that's the drama of this story, which is initiated before the Dresden High Court in May '35 as a group trial for preparation of high treason, but in fact merely plays out, unrolls like end credits written long before.

In the transcript of the court proceedings there are no roofs, no red paint, and all the city's letterboxes go empty. And no wonder, for the records show it was usually no more than a dozen flyers or newspapers that were passed from hand to hand per action, whereby plenty of them were burned by the young communists directly after, some even *before* being read, while other revolutionary print products found their homes in hallways or on windowsills, where they lived only brief lives, and even those pasted to fences or thrown over factory walls rarely elicited a response and never, not once, a single recruit.

And so they remained isolated and essentially alone, and instead of rallying with tens of thousands of comrades and shouting slogans, the young communists met in the forests around the city to hold what they called conspiratorial meetings, *assemblies*. There were usually only a handful of them present, and the only thing that still bore witness to the big wide world and the KPD's former standing was a few nameless couriers, who turned up on their motorcycles at the most impossible of hours and then disappeared again, leaving nothing but a couple of parcels of yearning, leaflets and printed matter bearing names like *Red Flag* or *Young Guard*.

And Hasso Grabner? According to his statement as recorded in the court transcript, he was deployed in the technical apparatus, but that too sounds so much bigger than it really was. Of the journals that he co-produced, often barely more than a hundred copies made their way into the world, and in some cases none at all, for there were times when Hasso Grabner failed to find whoever was supposed to distribute them. Then he would assume responsibility for his volatile freight, deposit it in a pigsty on the edge of town and try to find someone else to distribute it the day after.

Thus the story decodes itself, its banalities revealing a gaping chasm. Between the aims written down in the revolutionary publications and the scope of possibilities actually open to the illegally operating communists, is a gap as big as the history of their party. And yet Hasso Grabner and his 30 co-defendants are sentenced in May '35, their petty deeds – downright desperate-looking in retrospect – puffed up into gigantic plans for a coup.

For that is the other side of the story. Between the scope of possibilities open to Leipzig's young communists and the crimes written down in their indictments is a gap as big as the power of the National Socialist Party. And Hasso Grabner and his 30 co-defendants are shoved into just that gap.

In the logic of the Nazis, the story goes like this:

> Insofar as the defendants were involved in several separate crimes respectively, these were without exception merely dependent parts of an undertaking planned by them as a unit and appearing as such to the external observer. These separate crimes thus coalesce in the case of every defendant into a single prolonged act of preparation of high treason.

The guilty verdict is thereby merely a matter of form, the only surprise being the severity of the penalty. They slap a full four years on Hasso Grabner.

He could have got off with less. But because his appearance in court was just as confident as on the day when he burst through Max Altmann's office door, the judge gives him the full monty – and this time the door slams shut.

The City behind the Walls

On 3 May 1870, the wannabe writer Karl May* was transferred to the Waldheim house of correction. They slapped four years on him. He could have got off with less but he stole, cheated and tried his luck as a conman. Even during his arrest, he tried to tell the gendarmes another pack of lies, claiming he was the son of a rich plantation owner from the island of Martinique and had lost his papers on his trip to Europe. It took the authorities weeks to establish his true identity.

In Hasso Grabner's case, it all goes much faster. On his arrival at the station at precisely 2:10 p.m. on 28 May 1935, the guards already know who they're dealing with. Grabner is immediately handcuffed, loaded onto a cart, and horse-drawn to the house of correction through Waldheim, the 'pearl of the Zschopau Valley'.

On arrival he has to undress and is examined, numbered and showered. When he steps out of the washroom, he's standing before me. Hasso Grabner. 1.74 metres tall and 65 kilogrammes heavy. He's 23 years old, has a full head of brown hair and a large, straight nose in a slightly haggard face. His chin is wide, his mouth of normal size, his lips averagely curved. Behind them is a complete set of teeth. He looks quite healthy at first glance. His muscles are big and his bones are too. When he breathes in, he can extend his chest circumference to 93 centimetres, and when he breathes out there are still 81 centimetres left. He has no scars or tattoos, only a mole above the left corner of his mouth. His skin colour is white, his posture upright.

There he stands before me, dressing while the guards note everything down. One pair of underpants, one pair of socks, one shirt, one pair of trousers, one jacket and on his head a cap. Once he's finished dressing, his feet are kitted out with a pair of old shoes. Then Hasso Grabner gets the rest of his possessions. One comb, one mirror and the case containing his glasses. He is then led away. He wears a ring on one finger.

By the time Hasso Grabner enters his cell, Karl May is already there. He stole a fur in Leipzig, so he says, and that was the beginning of it all. Hasso Grabner says nothing. He looks in the mirror and sees his future floating away. It bobs downstream, along the Pleisse into the Mulde into the Zschopau. As Hasso Grabner fishes it out of the river there, Karl May is standing behind him and shrugs. Shortly afterwards, the cell door is opened, and Hasso Grabner is led away anew.

What follows is the intelligence test. Its purpose is to establish new arrivals' ability to work – and to maintain racial purity. Career criminals are sterilised, dangerous criminals are castrated, disabled criminals later euthanised. A single chit of paper suffices to have the prisoners sent 70 kilometres eastwards to Sonnenstein Castle, where they are gassed and cremated. But we haven't got that far yet. For now, it's Hasso Grabner's turn to take the intelligence test. The evaluator asks him questions. One of them is: 'Am I allowed to set my own house alight?'

More such gems follow. The Zschopau Valley is full of them:
'What is the difference between a staircase and a ladder?'
'What is 18 x 14?'
'Can you recite a poem?'

'Where is the easy life? Can anyone show it to you?'

The verdict is clear. Hasso Grabner is not only in perfect health; he is also intelligent and in possession of, as the evaluator notes, 'leadership qualities'. They'll soon get rid of those, though. In any case, Hasso Grabner can be used for any type of work at the house of correction; they can even send him out to the moor.

By the time Hasso Grabner returns to his cell after an hour and a half, Karl May has gone, and all he's left behind is a book. It's his autobiography. It would appear to originate from the prison library, although it's not quite clear whether Karl May smuggled his work in or out. No matter; the book is on the bed, and it contains the lines:

> I felt an irresistible urge to exploit the quiet and undisturbed cell for my intellectual progress as much as possible, and the officers revelled in assisting me in any way that did not contravene the institution's rules. Thus, my penal time was transformed into a time of study, during which greater composure and greater opportunities for immersion were available than a student ever encounters in freedom.

Hasso Grabner is surprised – and glad to read these words, having 'caught the education bug' a few months previously in remand custody, and it looks like he'll be able to cultivate it to the full extent in the Waldheim house of correction.

In actual fact, the old tradition from Karl May's days has survived. Once a week, the Waldheim inmates are served paper. They're all allowed to go to the prison library, borrow a book and then note down their thoughts as they read in their cells. The governor has exercise books issued to the prisoners especially for the purpose. The purpose of further education, as he says. To make sure prisoners don't educate themselves too much, however, the exercise books are checked regularly.

Hasso Grabner is given an exercise book too. But another man writes Grabner's name on its label. He's called Bruno Apitz*. Like Grabner, he is from Leipzig, a KPD member, and likewise imprisoned for high treason. And yet there is a difference between the two of them. Unlike Grabner, Apitz knows his father. He was an oilcloth printer. So it's no surprise that political prisoner Apitz writes a name label for political prisoner Grabner's blue oilcloth exercise book in the Waldheim house of correction.

From then on, Hasso Grabner fills his books with notes on natural history, psychology, politics and palaeontology. Between them, concealed, are little poems. Jail, of this Hasso Grabner is now certain, is the revolutionary's university.

Hasso Grabner would like to make a note of that. Like Karl May did. But he can't. The notebooks are examined on regular occasions, with draconic penalties for grammatical mistakes. And there is nowhere else to fix the thought, outside of his own head. In the first three months, no communication with the outside world is permitted. Even after that, prisoners are only granted one letter per month. All content is of course censored and any secret messages written in water, saliva, urine or milk are made visible using Wira-brand special solution.

And yet, even though it's difficult to make contact with the rest of the world and maintain it over the years, there are possibilities inside the house of correction. One thing is clear: anyone who regards communism as a form of asceticism finds plenty of fellow abstainers behind bars. So it's not long before Hasso Grabner discovers that the political prisoners held in Waldheim have set up a complex information system built upon secret messages through which the inmates communicate with each other. And Hasso Grabner already knows many of the men who tap coded missives from one side of a wall to the other, sending messages all the way across the prison.

There's Ernst Schneller, the fallen Communist Party functionary who taught him at the Rosa Luxemburg school back in 1930. And Fritz Selbmann, the former general secretary of Saxony's KPD, who had gone underground just like Grabner. And of course Georg Schumann, once a Central Committee member who served the Leipzig communists as political secretary.

But not only the incarcerated comrades have names; the staff have them too. And Hasso Grabner learns them before all the others: Wiederwill, Drescher, and Mordhorst – the head sergeant is called Against-Your-Will, the governor is Thrasher, and the next-door block is ruled over by the Murder-Nest sisters.

In Waldheim, of this Hasso Grabner is certain, names belong on gravestones.

The Mordhorst sisters rule the women's block. And there too, one of the inmates' name is Grabner. Waltraut Grabner was brought here back in 1933. There were a few months when she wasn't here. Because she had a baby. But now she's back, and she's kept her number, 129.

When Waltraut Grabner wants to speak to her husband she has to submit an application to the prison board and phrase her desire as a wish for a visit. Applications are only possible every few months. And in her case, they are still turned down every time. Only once, shortly before her release, does she receive a positive response, in January 1936:

> From: the Board of the Regional Penal Institution
> To: Prisoner 129/Grabner
> You are hereby granted a conversation with your husband, prisoner 801/Grabner, on a weekday, only on presentation of this letter, which is valid for one month.

The conversation lasts 20 minutes. Prisoners 129/Grabner and 801/Grabner are subsequently returned to their respective cells.

> I would like to mention another very impressive phenomenon: a door 'closed' itself at a distance of circa five metres from the medium. The light was always good, in some cases very bright.
>
> Conversation monitored. 10.55 – 11.15 a.m.
> Signed, Kühne

When his wife is released in February 1936, Hasso Grabner feels like he's half outside as well. 'My time,' he writes to her, 'is passing rapidly.' And yet there is a gap, the nine months in jail have torn a wound. And in it lies his son. Over and over in his letters, Grabner asks after the baby, and when he does get news of him he can't quite believe it.

'I must find my way back to an orderly way of life, come what may. I owe that to you and the boy,' he writes only days after his wife's release, and it sounds as though Hasso Grabner the communist is denying himself the revolution after only nine months behind bars. In future, so it seems, his life will revolve only around the family – and football.

Not that Hasso Grabner loves the sport that much, let alone plays it himself, or is even *capable* of playing it. In prison, though, he is employed as a ball-sewer, managing 'ten balls a week!' and predicting 'a great upswing for sport'. Why, he asks his wife, shouldn't they earn their living after his release by sewing balls?

But that's just an idea, perhaps nothing but a sop in the size and shape of a football. And – as such sops often are – shot more at his in-laws than at his wife. Hasso Grabner may be able to sew perfectly adequate balls. But in his heart, he remains a man whose favourite leather is the binding of books. And one day he can't help himself, one day he writes a letter to his in-laws and informs them of how he – and perhaps they too – sees things:

'Please don't think I want to be a semi-intellectual time-waster. Nor that I don't want to work.' And to make quite sure his dear parents-in-law understand him: 'I'm asking you to please give up your resistance to my reading material.'

To his wife, meanwhile, he sends a poem he's written, asking her for critique and critiquing it himself then and there.

'I didn't yet know about the strict rules of verse structure when I wrote it. I've got to know them in the meantime and my poems have been getting worse since then. Only when I liberate myself from them do I manage a good one now and then.'

And so the days pass, turn into weeks and grow into months, and Hasso Grabner, the untiring organiser, the high traitor and communist, dribbles the political ball but refrains from shooting, reads not Karl Marx but Karl May, and writes love poems rather than agitprop.

Have they domesticated him? Driven the spectre of communism out of him? In one of his last letters, Grabner himself wrote: 'A man whose actions are always along the same lines is either as dull as a stick or a mature personality.'

What he didn't write, however, is what to call a mixture of dull and mature. The answer would have been very simple: a pragmatist. And Hasso Grabner is pragmatic through and through.

Pragmatism is the basic ingredient of his story. Communist ideology is the form in which it expresses itself. Here, though, in the Waldheim house of correction, it can't express itself openly; it's not allowed to. So it has to seek other paths. The fact that it does so in footballs, adventure novels and love poems is part of the story. The fact that it doesn't get lost along the way is due not only to the KPD functionaries imprisoned along with Hasso Grabner, but also to the Nazis, who arrest more and more communists and put them into Waldheim. After 1936, the prison board is no longer able to exclude the political prisoners from certain functions.

And so political propagandists become packers, district chairmen become dispensary assistants, and local secretaries become librarians. They all send secret messages, pass on secret messages, receive secret messages. Staunch socialists conspire. Subversive slammer standards.

But still, life in Waldheim isn't easy. Certainly not when you have to sew balls for ten hours a day under strict supervision while forbidden to speak, and spend the rest of the time in a cell with hardened criminals. One of the latter, however, stands out. He writes poems. And his communist cellmate gets to read them.

> These poems were no works of art, as the prisoner in question had no idea of metre and verse structure, but put his poems together more or less according to his feelings. In the poems, he now expressed his thoughts on fascism. Despite his criminal tendencies, he was essentially aware of his proletarian existence. He was therefore also aware that his poetic products had a subversive character under fascist law. Hence, he hid them in the lining of the hand mirror he kept in his locker.

They are eventually found there, the criminal prisoner is indicted, and the communist is called as a witness. Only by coincidence does he realise that the poetry is only a pretext and the defendant a mere mock defendant, a decoy to make the caged communist sing.

To cut a long story short: Hasso Grabner plays neither the stool pigeon nor the hero, and when he's released on 14 August 1938 after 1,475 days behind bars and the prison gates close behind him, he is a free man for precisely five seconds. Then a Gestapo officer walks up to him, cuffs him and takes him to Buchenwald concentration camp outside Weimar.

From: Gestapo Leipzig
Re: Release of Prisoner 801/Grabner
Hereby request evaluation of need for possible subsequent surveillance in accordance with circular decree issued by Reich Justice Minister as of 18 January 1937.

From: Governing Board of Waldheim House of Correction
Re: Release of 801/Grabner
The unclear nature of his character and the return to his wife make him at least politically at risk. We therefore consider surveillance imperative with regard to his contacts and those of his wife to politically suspicious persons and must advise such surveillance.

From: Gestapo / Police Leipzig ref. II-D-288/38
To: the Governor of Waldheim House of Correction
Re: Hasso Benno Grabner, born 21.10.1911 in Leipzig, resident in Leipzig-Schönefeld
Reference: Release report no. 801
Request the transfer of the prisoner Grabner, due for release on 14.8.1938, by collective transport to the local police prison.
Leipzig, 6.8.1938
Signed p.p.: Verlohren

To: the United Penal Institution Waldheim/Saxony
Re: Defendant no. 801/21 Hasso Grabner
I hereby politely request information on which train my husband will be using on Sunday and what time he will be released, as I should like to pick him up if possible.

Hasso Grabner takes the train from Waldheim via Chemnitz and Glauchau to Weimar. Because his guard works up the kind of appetite that a communist can't staunch, however, they go to an inn on the way. There, Hasso Grabner manages to hand his exercise books from the house of correction to the landlord, unnoticed. It is a stab in the dark. The two men don't know each other. The only tie between them is a searching look – and the address of a woman in Leipzig, which Hasso Grabner dashes down on a scrap of paper. A few days later, the woman receives a parcel. It contains dozens of notepads, full of handwriting – the product of Hasso Grabner's hunger for education, the payment for being served paper in Waldheim.

Weimar

When Hasso Grabner arrives in Buchenwald at 6 p.m. sharp on 25 August 1938, Karl May is the only one missing. All the others are there. Bruno Apitz, for example, the exercise book-labeller from Waldheim. Or Willi Seifert*, a bricklayer by trade who also made the acquaintance of the pearl of the Zschopau Valley but, being a KPD man, only got to see the walls of the house of correction from the inside. Not to forget Albert Kuntz*, who everyone in Buchenwald calls Kuntze, and who comes from Saxony just like Grabner and served the state's communists as a functionary. They're all there and watch Hasso Grabner being brought in to the camp – what they don't know is that he's been there before.

Flashback. Exit the Gestapo – enter Goethe. Or at least what's left of him…

The year is 1928, and Hasso Grabner, just turned 17, takes the train from Leipzig to Weimar with a group of young communists to pay a visit to Goethe's house. The future revolutionaries spend hours in the poet's former home, inspecting paper and pens, ink and bones, and while most of them gradually see their fill, start to get hungry and leave, Hasso Grabner stays behind. He stands rapt at the display cases, gets caught up in reading the manuscripts on display and immerses himself deeply – so deeply that at some point he fades out of view. At least no once notices him when the building closes. Overnight, however, Goethe's ghost must have materialised and the next morning taken on the earthly form of a young man, with not the poet's collected works on his person but a Communist Party membership book, which agitates the staff into calling the police and having the intruder arrested. Once it becomes clear that nothing has been stolen, nothing is damaged and everything is still exactly as Goethe left it, Hasso Grabner is set free and sent back to Leipzig.

In 1938, he's back in the Weimar area. And meets, in the concentration camp, his communist comrades of yore, now 10 years older. Knowing he's so keen on Goethe, they get him a job in the camp library; it contains pretty much all of the poet's works.

'Sometimes I read as well,' Grabner writes to his wife, and who knows, perhaps the friendly, inviting interior of the concentration-camp library even reminds him a little of Goethe's former home not far away...

> The long library room was bright and clean. The pale-painted bookshelves along the walls and in the middle of the room were a pleasant surprise, likewise the tightly packed, neatly bound books with their black-and-white labels on the spines, the green and red of the geraniums outside the windows and the cacti climbing along the shelves.

Is it alright to write that? Is it alright to write it *like that*? Or perhaps one ought to write like this:

> GDR Ministry of State Security, Archive No. 3958/62, re: Hasso Grabner
> Grabner played an inglorious role during the fascist era by insinuating himself into a special position in Buchenwald concentration camp and encapsulating himself from the other comrades. Signed: Fischer, Ltn

He's right, that Stasi lieutenant, the camp library at Buchenwald really is a capsule. But it's much more than that. It's a capsule inside a capsule. And the only thing that distinguishes the two capsules is the fact that the outer one is surrounded by SS men and an electrically charged barbed-wire fence, while the inner one is surrounded by prisoners and their desire for books.

In the middle of the inner capsule, however, in the room with the geraniums and cacti, is Hasso Grabner. His comrades got him the job there at the end of '38, after four months on one of the murderous outside labour crews. The Goethe bit was just a pretext, of course; Goethe is dead. But they, the comrades, want to live. And to do so, they need the dead, they need their books and their writing. Not only to indulge their communist education addiction, but also to exchange thoughts, views and opinions and not lose their own standpoint amidst the camp's arbitrariness. That's why they got Hasso Grabner the library job. Because he's a bookseller. And a communist. And because the men who bunk with him in Block 38 – Neubauer, Stoecker and Kuntze – are also kapos*, prisoner functionaries entitled to make suggestions to the SS. But that wouldn't suffice, wouldn't be nearly enough, if they couldn't also persuade the other political prisoners of Grabner's suitability. They can do precisely that, though, because as Saxon communists they are the leading faction in the camp. They're the only ones able to hold together the fragmented KPD's many local branches and coordinate their actions. And yet in the end it is the SS who decide; neither the Saxon communists nor Hasso Grabner can do a thing about that.

The camp management's acceptance of the suggestion to put Grabner in the library was not down to his bookselling talents, it seems, but due to the plain and simple fact that Grabner is a common-or-garden communist in the eyes of the SS, a mid-level functionary, a second-class hero, a man who meets his Waterloo not in an outside labour crew but in front of a bookshelf, facing the 62 copies of Hitler's *Mein Kampf* purchased by the SS specifically for the concentration-camp library.

There he stands, Hasso Grabner, in his frayed zebra suit, in the middle of the inner capsule, in the room with the 62 Adolfs. Behind him on the shelf is Goethe's *Wilhelm Meister's Apprenticeship*; his own epic journeyman's years lie ahead of him. But Hasso Grabner has no time for Goethe now. He much prefers to admire the green and red geraniums in the windows, gaze at the exotic, even adventurous-looking cacti – and think back to Karl May. Wasn't he employed in the prisoners' library as well? Back then, in Waldheim? And wasn't he in charge of lending, just like Grabner?

On 1 March 1874, a Sunday, the prisoner Karl Julius Hering returns a book to the prison library in the Waldheim house of correction. Two days later, the library administrator, the Protestant catechist August Leopold Barth, establishes via a routine check that the book has been dirtied. The library worker Karl May, who signed out the book, is questioned on the matter but defends Hering and declares that the book was already dirty when he lent it out. Hering himself has nothing to say on the issue, but states on further enquiry from Barth, 'he believes the book was clean when he got it. He says he did not dirty it.'

No big deal, essentially. Especially not something for which Prisoner 401/Karl May is responsible. He is nonetheless discharged from library service. Hering, however, who would appear to have mucked up the book despite not believing he did, gets away scot free.

Sixty-five years later, Grabner inspects every book returned to the Buchenwald concentration-camp library, examines them for stains, rips and marginalia. Any abnormalities, the SS instruct him, are to be noted down on the book's back endpaper, ignoring the question of deliberate intent. The prisoner is then banned from reading, either way. And placed under strict arrest. And given a beating if he objects. One blow of the cane per word spoken.

Hasso Grabner knows he can't change that. He sits inside the capsule, with the prisoners crowding around the lending counter outside. They are not allowed in. The books are passed from inside to outside. Inside, where Hasso Grabner sits in the warm, is Block 4, one of the few camp buildings the SS has fitted with heating. It wouldn't do to let the Führer freeze over, 62 times every winter.

Outside in the camp, however, it is bitterly cold. A keen west wind is almost always blowing across the slopes of the Ettersberg. It blows on this day too, 13 January 1939, when a sudden whistle sounds, scattering the cluster around Hasso Grabner's lending counter in a matter of seconds. What has happened?

Walter Wolf reports: 'Another career criminal had escaped, and the entire camp had to stand for eight or ten hours in a snowstorm, at 20 degrees below zero. Our unforgettable comrade Walter Stoecker came to us and said: "You were the last to read Lenin's *Empirio-Criticism*, now tell us what you remember of it."'

Is that feasible? Reading Lenin, in Buchenwald? It must be a communist tall tale. And yet, the book really was there, according to the camp archive, smuggled in hidden in a medicine case. Lenin is not in Grabner's library though. Afraid of the book being discovered, the communists hand it around a small circle of comrades to 'begin intensive theoretical training'.

And then they present the results in a snowstorm during a punishment roll call in a concentration camp?

'The communists used every possible opportunity to refresh their theoretical knowledge,' says Walter Wolf.

'That may well be,' say I, 'but it still sounds like a tall tale to me.'

But Walter Wolf ignores me and goes on with his story.

'In that snowstorm, with chattering teeth, in the bleak misery of the concentration camp, we found in the thoughts of Lenin, in the

Marxist truth of that great philosopher and statesman, the inner strength to understand the greatness and significance of Lenin's words: "The Marxist doctrine is omnipotent because it is true."'

Sixty-five years later, Hasso Grabner's widow writes to me that her husband 'only ever told unheroic or even funny stories from the camp.'

She doesn't mention a comrade by the name of Walter Stoecker, and the only place where I come across Walter Stoecker, former delegate to the World Congress of the Communist International, in conjunction with Hasso Grabner, is an unremarkable file in the Saxon State Archive in Leipzig. It is one of the many narrative curricula vitae written by Grabner, in which Stoecker appears as one of the 'four friends' who got him out of the hell of the outside labour crew and into the barrack with the books, telling him his task from then on was to find a few pages of paradise among all the Nazi pulp.

And Hasso Grabner really does find them. In February 1939, he discovers a book by a Jew named Heine. The writer's first name is as German as it gets – Heinrich. Yet that's not the reason why the book is in the library – good old Heinrich is an enemy of the state, as are all those who possess his books. The Nazis outside in Germany didn't confiscate his complete works for nothing, after all. The plan was to pulp the books, but a portion of them – how, no one can say – has ended up in Buchenwald, where they are to be ripped up and made into toilet paper.

Those selected for this labour know their Heine well, however. They know this is their chance for a little *Winter's Tale* – and before you can say *Atta Troll*, good old Heinrich is removed by the shithouse crew and slotted into Hasso Grabner's library.

When the Kommandoführer comes on his rounds, of course, the book vanishes. His name – how could it be any other way? – is

Thorwächter, meaning gatekeeper. Kurt Thorwächter, to be precise. Being an SS-Oberscharführer, he pays little attention to the library, however. At most, he's interested in the adjacent book-binding workshop, where two dozen prisoners carry out private commissions on his behalf. Beyond that, he has little time for paperwork and is generally known in the camp as a friend of more solid artforms. For his 30th birthday, Kurt Thorwächter orders his prisoners to make him a large wooden platter on the lathe, spelling out KURT THORWÄCHTER in thickly carved letters around the brim.

And yet, as guileless as gatekeeper Thorwächter may be, there is no way out of the camp for the prisoners. They will remain behind the fence, so it seems, until the final victory, living in their cold, crowded barracks until the Day of Nazi Judgement. No wonder one of the most-borrowed books in Grabner's concentration camp library is Gustav Adolf Platz's *Wohnräume der Gegenwart*. Who wouldn't want to read about more comfortable contemporary living spaces? All other desires are quenched by atlases, travel literature and fiction.

Once the winter is over, Walter Stoecker dies. The SS made him wheel barrows full of shit for months on end, and then camp physician Dr Ding jabbed his injections into him. Officially, though, Stoecker dies of typhus. Hasso Grabner accompanies him on his last journey. On 11 March 1939, Walter Stoecker is cremated to a crisp in Goethe's Weimar.

And thus time passes. And with it, lives. One after another. And while 802 died in 1938, the Buchenwald statistics count 1378 corpses a year later. Essentially, however, that is merely the overture, history warming up, the backstory to the great slaughter.

As of 24 August 1939, Hitler and Stalin make a pact. The German invasion of Poland begins on 1 September, expanding into a world war. On 17 September, Soviet troops occupy eastern Poland. Eleven days later, on 28 September, Ribbentrop and Molotov sign the German-Soviet Frontier and Friendship Treaty in Moscow. Some 40,000 Polish civilians are murdered during the first month of the war. As of 1 October, the library at Buchenwald has a stock of 5582 volumes.

Outside, in the barracks, in the inner spaces of the large capsule, the lines are meanwhile beginning to tangle. As a result of the war, more and more prisoners are being brought to the camp, and with them comes information, so much information that the communists at some point stop knowing where the enemy stands. They don't even know who the enemy is. And yet it used to be clear-cut. The enemy was the social democrats. And the national socialists, obviously. But essentially, they were one and the same in the eyes of the communist leaders, the SPD merely the left hand of the Nazis, 'the moderate wing of fascism', and thus the fight was to be fought 'not jointly with the Social Democratic Party, but against it'.

That was the party line. With that line in mind, the communists went into illegality in the early 30s and from there into the prisons, houses of correction and concentration camps. For a long time, many communists in Buchenwald were *absolutely unaware* that Comintern, the international communist organisation, had not regarded Social Democracy as an opponent since 1935, nor that in the meantime the German Communist Party leadership had announced its anti-fascist popular-front policy – at a party conference held in Moscow exile but given the cover name of the 'Brussels Conference'. Those now bringing this information into the camp from outside soon find themselves in the role of heretics sowing disbelief. The result is endless heated debates, in which the disciples of the Great Church of Communism concentrated in the camp only slowly realise that the devil's brood of social democrats are now part of the heavenly host of anti-Hitler activism.

Then, barely has the thing about the popular front been believed and accepted for better or worse, the next lot come to Buchenwald and share the news of the Molotov-Ribbentrop Pact and that Stalin has been handing German communists over to the Third Reich for years. The communists in the camp are now utterly confused and have to abandon their newly acquired belief in the popular front, whether they like it or not, and regard the line drawn down the middle of Poland as a peaceable frontier between two perhaps not friendly, but non-aggressive nations, while the social democrats, who according to Stalin are actually the twin brothers of the fascists, are now no longer part of the alliance, which prompts the latter to start calling the communists, in turn, 'red-painted doubles of the Nazis'.

And Hasso Grabner? He keeps out of all the discussions criss-crossing the camp (and the camps in the camp), works his shifts in the library, waters the geraniums, pricks his arms and legs on the coarse cacti and gets an entry in his Stasi file for his pains 23 years later.

He can't possibly know (and even if he suspected, he wouldn't believe it) that the resolution and manifesto of the KPD's Brussels Conference, which would provide clarification to the political discussions and ease the heated mood among the prisoners, is printed with a fake cover bearing the title *How to Take Correct Care of Our Cacti*.

Only 11 by 8 cm, the booklet was smuggled into Lichtenburg concentration camp by Walter Stoecker in 1936. When the Lichtenburg camp was wound down in August 1937, the books were brought to Buchenwald and formed the foundation of the library. The cacti book seems not to have made the journey. Or at least I can't find it anywhere in Buchenwald now, three quarters of a century later, and it makes no appearance in the catalogue published in the camp library on 1 October 1939. But why should it?

It's a fake book. Walter Stoecker, who got hold of it, is no longer alive by this point – and all that remains is a dozen entirely un-fake cacti leaning against the shelves, their spikes conducive to anything but clarifying and easing the situation.

And thus ends year '39, and number 40 begins. Hasso Grabner is now 28. Short of a miracle, he will spend his birthday – number 40 – in the camp.

On New Year's Eve of 1939, Hasso Grabner is sitting in Block 38 and thinking of his wife. And his son. 'I can still barely believe he's now marching through life with a school satchel on his back,' he writes to her. And then: 'For us, for our son, for our happiness, these two words describe our mission: solidarity and perseverance.'

The pragmatist in him is clearly an optimist. Not a trace of self-pity. 'Not only because it wouldn't help, no, but because it does not conform to my innermost self. Perhaps it's the case that a man misses that which he loves most the least, because his strength of feeling, the ardency of his love, does not permit him to regard spatial separation as the essential factor, or even merely as *an* essential factor.' And then: 'I admit there is a possibility that this thought is mental self-defence, because one couldn't bear it otherwise, but it exists and is without a doubt effective.'

Another thing that's without a doubt is that the role of librarian is a very welcome one for Hasso Grabner the bookseller, because not only can he now read and provide his pals with publications, he can also have conversations and hear stories. Like the one about the French prisoner who makes the SS officers green with envy with his family tree dating back to the 13th century. Or the one about the *Völkischer Beobachter*, which a number of inmates particularly enjoy borrowing. Not to read it, of course; when it's cold outside and the icy wind whistles across the camp, the Nazi party newspaper makes an excellent insulation layer underneath a prison uniform.

Grabner even meets a real-life writer at the camp library. He is a man named Steinitz, who has written a novel about the altar maker Tilman Riemenschneider. Being of Jewish origin, however, Steinitz was forced to publish his book under the pseudonym Karl Heinrich Stein and hope no one would notice the masquerade. And by Jove, it worked! No one worked out that the work was written by an *'Untermensch**, and the Nazi press went as far as praising the book to the skies. Even the *Völkischer Beobachter* celebrated it.

That was in 1936. Now, though, four years later, Steinitz finds himself in Buchenwald concentration camp – and shortly after that, finds his own book in the camp library. Hasso Grabner is a little confused by the whole crazy story. To Steinitz, however, it's absolutely clear what's happening.

'One of us doesn't belong here,' he informs the baffled SS a few days after the book is discovered, 'the novel or me.'

The SS plumps for Steinitz. He is placed on a list, sent away and gassed in Auschwitz in 1942.

Hasso Grabner also ends up on a list, but this one is written by the communists. It's a list of prisoners suggested for release – and protective-custody Prisoner 5334/Grabner is accepted by the SS.

The big day comes on 24 June 1940. Another 14 prisoners are released alongside Hasso Grabner. There are no new arrivals on that date, but a few men considered unworthy of bearing arms plus a number of Poles and Jews do 'perish' in the camp or are shot dead 'attempting escape'.

On the evening of 24 June, shortly after 6 p.m., Hasso Grabner leaves Buchenwald to enter a new form of captivity outside the camp.

Leaving

To leave the concentration camp, Hasso Grabner has to sign a declaration of loyalty. To be allowed to work as a bookseller again, he is now supposed to write a plea for mercy to Goebbels' Reich Chamber of Literature and ask for admission. But Grabner doesn't ask. And he refuses to be asked. He's had enough of books and Buchenwald. And so, Hasso Grabner the bookseller abdicates and becomes a labourer in a Leipzig factory. The resistance fighter in him remains, however, and seeks an opportunity to do something – and one day he finds it.

In April 1941, Grabner finds employment in a production firm and is promoted to works manager a few months later. The boilers the company manufactures play a part in the smooth running of the German war machinery, that much he knows. Fuelling that machine is not an option for the communist Hasso Grabner, yet stopping it is impossible. There seems to be no space between the two. And if there is, then only a few millimetres. Perhaps that's enough, though, perhaps the odd part might break a little sooner if it deviates from its planned measurements by a few millimetres…

What Hasso Grabner is doing is sabotaging the arms industry; he's aware of that. A little every day, inconspicuous, its end effect invisible to him. In the best case there'll be hope, in the worst case a hanging. In the gargantuan works of the German war machinery, the resistance fighter Hasso Grabner takes on the powerful role of a single spanner, realising every day anew that it would take a whole battery of toolboxes to stop the machinery for even a second.

In October '42, however, times change. The fascist campaign of destruction has ground to a halt, and Hitler's Wehrmacht grants Hasso Grabner, previously labelled unworthy of bearing arms, the 'opportunity' to prove himself on the frontlines. Grabner is drafted into a 999th penal battalion* and allocated to the Africa Brigade. First of all, though, it's off to Baden-Württemberg, to the Heuberg, a desolate 900-metre hill where it's winter for nine months of the year and cold for the other three. There, on the grounds of a former concentration camp, a parade ground has been set up as a whetstone for men unworthy of bearing arms. And those who refuse to be set up are ground down. By the Wehrmacht teams training them, who miss no opportunity to bully the new arrivals and show them they must fall in line when 'the Führer generously grants them a unique opportunity to become fully valued soldiers and citizens once again, through their own achievements and good behaviour.'

Those fully valued soldiers on the Heuberg hill... Some wear uniforms from the First World War because new ones are not available. Others have jackets from the current war, strewn with bullet holes and stained with the blood of the fallen. In the early days even plates and cutlery are in short supply on the Heuberg. If the men want to eat, they take off their hats and get their rations slopped in, spooning them up with their bare hands. Not until shortly before their departure for Belgium in December 1942 does the situation improve. Instead of half-raw frostbitten potatoes, there are suddenly proper meals. The reason is as simple as it is banal: emaciated members of the master race don't make a good impression in an occupied country.

On arrival in Belgium, Grabner tries to maintain contact with his comrades from the Heuberg and get an overview of the situation on the ground with the aid of locals. Little more is possible. It's hard enough to do conspiratorial work in the penal company.

The freshly trained gunner Hasso Grabner is reallocated a full five times within the troop to keep him from exerting a political influence over the 'regular' soldiers. But the other communists are also reserved about taking actions. And that's wise of them, because even the smallest of misdemeanours spell death. Soldiers in the penal battalion are executed for petty trifles; comrades are forced to stand in infantry squares around a row of wooden posts onto which "unworthy" soldiers are tied before their lives are taken by the firing-squad rifles.

For those who survive, however, Belgium is a mere stop along the way; the destination is Africa. The Allied troops there are driving a sandman named Rommel ahead of them and are threatening to cast him into the sea in Tunisia.

It's a long road to Africa, though. In February and March of '43, that road takes Hasso Grabner via Avignon and Nîmes on to Monaco and Rome, where the Pope himself protests against Grabner and co., seeing them as a danger to honourable Italian soldiers.

The Wehrmacht commanders don't give a papal fig, as is to be expected. They send the penal battalion on from Rome to Naples. Along the way, Grabner and his comrades keep getting caught between the fronts; the German communists in Wehrmacht uniform killed by Italian resistance bombs, shot at by Allied planes and executed by their 'own' officers for subversion of the war effort or attempted desertion.

For those who make it through, the journey reveals itself on 5 April 1943 to be a suicide mission escorted by friendly fire. On that date, parts of the 3rd and 4th company of the 1st Africa Battalion are loaded onto 15 Junkers Ju 52 transport planes at Naples airport and flown directly to Tunis. The coast of Africa is in sight when British fighter pilots make a sudden appearance and attack the low-flying Axis aircraft. The soldiers inside see their attackers reflected in the water below them. Then the bombs rain down over them as they speed only 20 metres above the sea. When the planes attempt to climb higher, the British aircraft canons start firing. 'Most of us don't dare look out of the window.' Those who do get shot in the face. The Junkers soon drop to the water as burning torches, extinguishing themselves. Dozens die. 'The sea is covered with floating aircraft remains, gurgling to the bottom.'

Hasso Grabner is lucky, though. A few days before the planes' departure, the commandant of the fourth battery of the Africa Infantry Regiment 962 took him aside and told him straight out: 'Grabner, in Europe I have the Führer with his power behind me, in Africa I'd be standing alone against you.' The result being that instead of being put on a plane, Hasso Grabner is put in the bread-thief company with petty criminals, and returns outwardly unharmed via Italy and Austria to the Heuberg in good old Swabia. The rest of the 962nd Regiment, meanwhile, dies an overheated death outside Tunis.

So there he is, Hasso Grabner, dishonourably discharged, then drafted and then discarded again. Certainly unworthy of bearing arms for the Nazis. Back on the Heuberg with no idea what to do. But he's not the only one; the Wehrmacht commanders have no idea either what to do with a man like him. All they know is that a communist in their ranks is a risk, even if he's in the Wehrmacht's own uniform. Then again, if the man's already got his tropical equipment he might as well be sent out again. He certainly won't need it on the Heuberg – they don't call the local town Stetten on Cold Arse for nothing.

And so on it goes, and while Hasso Grabner sits alone and lonesome in one of the barracks and waits for a decision on his further fate, the Heuberg outside his window suddenly gets crowded.

Hundreds of soldiers return from the penal battalion. Most of them were disarmed in Italy for fear of a mutiny, stuck in cattle trucks and sent 'home' by train to the Swabian whetstone.

But they don't stay for long. The first 999ers leave the Heuberg again as early as May '43. Where they're heading, they don't know. The train they're on takes an unfamiliar route and makes slow progress. The hours pass, turning to days. At some point the soldiers realise they're travelling south-eastwards. Some try to escape, others enjoy the view. When they get to the mountains, low cars full of gravel are connected up in front of the locomotive. A purely precautionary measure, they're told.

During the night, though, flares are fired into the sky and bathe the valley through which the train is passing in glowing white light. Soon afterwards shots fall, the roar of battle, machine-gun fire, screams. Then quiet. A hospital train pulls up beside them at some point, taking the parallel tracks for a while. The soldiers see wounded men lying in the brightly lit compartments. By the time they spot bodies dangling from telegraph poles the next day, they are in Serbia. Next come Albania, Greece and a ship in Piraeus harbour, the crew explaining they should be prepared to be torpedoed by British submarines.

What kind of times are these,
when pigs feast on freshly slaughtered men?

Hasso Grabner, *The Cell* (novel)

Greek History – An Outline

Greek history is a bumpy ride. That's common knowledge. But this is extreme.

It is 12 October 1940, and Mussolini is angry. 'Hitler keeps presenting me with one *fait accompli* after another!' the Duce complains after the Wehrmacht has gone and invaded Romania without asking – when Mussolini wanted to be the first to launch a raid on a country for once. Admittedly, he did do that with Albania a year and a half previously on 7 April '39, but Albania is Albania, and the only things you can do there are herd goats and pick your nose.

Mussolini's foreign minister – young, ambitious and blessed with the name of Galeazzo Ciano – has another idea, though, and suggests to Mussolini that they annex Greece. It's an easy victory, he says. All they have to do is build a few nice wide roads from Albania into Hellas and meanwhile stir up a bit of unrest over in Greece, so that there's not only a way in but also a reason to impose order down there.

The Duce likes the idea. 'All roads lead to Athens,' says the Roman, and gives the foreign minister – who also happens to be his son-in-law – *carte blanche* to bring Albania up to date in terms of road traffic and to look for a pretext to light the fuse in Greece.

Once he's found one, Mussolini is delighted, but his first thought is of Hitler. 'This time I'll pay him back in his own coin. He'll find out I've invaded Greece from the newspapers.' And lo and behold, on 28 October the fuse is lit, and while Hitler is on board Himmler's special train, which goes by the name of 'Heinrich', reading the paper on his way to Florence, the Italian fascists invade Greece – disguised as firemen.

Two weeks later, admittedly, their own plans go up in flames, because the Greeks make a counterstrike and push back the Italians, whereupon Mussolini establishes, in the spring of '41: 'We have not made a single step of progress.'

In Berlin, meanwhile, Hitler is getting a kick out of watching Ciano and co. 'burning their noses' – and promptly invades Greece himself, which lays down its arms on 20 April, *his birthday!* But that's just the start of the drama. Because although the Greeks have beaten the Italians and surrender solely and exclusively to the Germans, Mussolini demands that the history books shall state 'surrender to the Italians', which enrages not only the Greek generals but also their German counterparts to such an extent that both groups go out for a demonstrative dinner together, leaving the Italians behind on their ownsome in the next best taverna with their freshly written capitulation contract and an empty history book.

And so it goes on. One lot makes history and the others rewrite it, and to make matters nice and complicated, the Brits soon enter the arena and offer a London sanctuary to the Greek king, evacuated to Egypt, which the latter welcomes wholeheartedly, seeing as he feels like an Englishman anyway and is otherwise 'a loveable idiot with no feelings whatsoever for Greece, its people or its politicians'. Ideal qualities, in other words, for drinking tea in London, giving good advice and letting the Brits ply him with medals, including the Distinguished Service Order for meritorious wartime service, for bravery during his escape.

There's more. The Germans occupy (and maltreat) the land, the Italians tell everyone who wants to hear (or doesn't) about 'their' conquest and the Brits delight in the role of agents on his majesty's secret service.

And the Greeks? They start organising resistance, founding such a large number of liberation groups for the purpose that even the British agents swarming the country lose count and can no longer distinguish between ELAS, EDES, EAM, PEAN, ESPO and ESON, not to mention the differences between ESA, ESAS and ESAP.

The groups themselves don't give an antifascist fig; they keep on merrily forming new alliances – though not always against the enemy, but increasingly against one another. So it's no great surprise that at some point all the combination options of the alphabet have been used up, and what's more, resistance groups with the exact same name have arisen that hate each other more than they jointly abhor the Germans.

Hence (among other things) the fight raged between EDES and EDES the turncoats, whereby both sides claim to be on the right side and accuse the other of collaborating with the Germans, who in turn see not only no possibility, but also 'no reason' to differentiate, and instead praise the 'Athens EDES leadership's good cooperation with German command posts', which is only consequential in a way, as the German command posts are the only bodies that can match the Greek resistance groups in terms of quantity (in pure numbers) and quality (of confusion of competencies). 'As early as October 1943, there are 161 competing German command posts in Athens alone.'

No wonder one of them is in touch with the EDES leadership, even though the Germans don't always know exactly who's behind the name and can't distinguish the right EDES from the *right* EDES, and the only possibility to trigger something like a separation of EDES and EDES from outside is to ask oneself (but certainly not the Greeks!) which of the two is actually *fighting* – fighting the Germans, not each other.

At any rate, most of the Greek resistance groups, above all those from the bourgeois royalist camp, merely make the Germans into meatloaf verbally, on top of which they have no members – apart from their five leaders – though that doesn't stop them from writing policy papers full of philological sophistications as they slowly go to pot in various Athens coffee houses, fully believing the waiters fawning around them to be collaborators.

It's absolutely logical in such a climate that even archbishops would begin to write military statements, begging God or at least the British Foreign Office to let parachutists rain from the sky. And lo, their calls are heard, and it's not long before the clouds above Greece start raining British liaison officers – first a light sprinkling, then more and more – not only carrying a significant number of gold sovereigns on their persons, but also jumping from planes that dump weapons, ammunition and clothing all over the country. Admittedly in one case, all that falls from the sky is 22 left boots, but that's no reason to complain because, as everyone in Greece knows, the Lord moves in ways as mysterious as the British Foreign Office.

In any case Greece, torn to pieces by its own people, its geography and the German Wehrmacht units, is soon better connected, with the aid of the British liaison officers, than Mussolini's Albanian enclave to Athens, and only the speed with which the British agents wander the Greek peninsula, meet known and unknown groups and write corresponding memoranda keeps them from following good old Lord Elgin's example and stuffing their suitcases with beautifully decorated slabs of marble.

And so it goes on. The Germans occupy the land, the Greeks defend it in the rugged peaks and public houses, and the Brits fancy themselves as the ones pulling the strings in the puppet theatre.

And the Italians?

They do go on fighting a bit, but no one can fail to notice that the majority of the Italian soldiers are more interested in wardrobe issues than warfare, so that everyone (and presumably the Italian soldiers most of all) realises the Greek partisans will disarm them sooner or later. 'The contrast between the Italians' impeccably ironed uniforms and good shoes and the ragged barefoot partisans was simply too great.'

Whereby being a partisan in general and disarming Italians in particular is not so simple for the Greeks, or at least *wasn't* at the beginning of the war, when the most combative of their generals decided to turn themselves into guerrillas, but noticed after a while that they understood next to nothing about that kind of warfare, having learned nothing whatsoever about it at the Athens military academy, due to the simple fact that the publishers of the Greek translation of Clausewitz's textbook *On War* considered the chapter on partisans superfluous and printed the book without it.

The Greek generals were thus useless in the resistance struggle from the very beginning, and it has fallen to the simple folk to camp out in the mountains and shoot at Germans, Italians or other Greeks.

There are certainly plenty of opportunities for shooting, and if not, then they're simply invented, while the remains of the Greek army are condemned to idleness in their own land. The majority of the officers command nothing more than date trees or are sitting around – following the German example – in some command post or other, their functions unknown even to the London Foreign Office.

And the rest of the formerly glorious troops? The Greek navy in its Cairo exile, for instance, what are they up to?

The historians answer like this: 'Among all ranks, card games soon become almost the most respectable leisure activity, with leisure becoming the rule. Otherwise, smuggling, 'brothel service', drinking and knife fights dance a merry round. Weapons and equipment are stolen *en masse* and hawked to Arabs and Zionists.' Others prefer setting up drug rings or let themselves get put in charge of a dubious Egyptian prison – what else is there to do? – and then have all the fun of duping the British inspectors by importing hashish by the tonne from Palestine. That's not even the half of it. If the Greek king can't stand the Greeks, the Greek navy can despise the water. In other words: 'Many officers spend most of their time on land and bring their female playmates on board at all hours of the day and night, recruiting a "band" from their own crew to complete the Dionysian triptych with its melodic component.'

No wonder a third of them are soon suffering from venereal diseases.

Then again, things look rather similar back home in Athens, except in this case it's the Germans getting syphilis. Or to be precise, getting given syphilis, as the Greek resistance takes place not only in the rugged peaks and public houses, but also in private. The brothel owners of Athens know precisely which of their girls have syphilis and deliberately couple them up with the Germans – and they couple so often and freely that Rommel starts complaining he gets nothing but 'rotted' soldiers.

Now, *that's* a problem the communist resistance fighters among the Greeks don't have, just for once, what with them practicing their legendary abstinence even in the rugged peaks. Meanwhile, in a moment of weakness and dressed only in short trousers, the exiled king deigns to receive a delegation of the National Liberation Front in Cairo ('over fruit salad'), and explains to the astounded partisan representatives: 'I have heard a great deal about your little mountain antics.'

Unaware of any antics, the communist functionaries' jaws drop, and only later does it become clear it was down to the king's lousy Greek and he meant not 'antics' (*kamōmata*) but 'achievements' (*katorthōmata*).

And so it goes on, in a messy mix of against and alongside one another, and the years trot carelessly by, and at some point the number of people losing their lives in the whole performance is of no more interest to anyone. 'They had preserved the dead like fruit, and the harvest was good.'

And Mussolini, the starting point of this sketched Greek history? He is toppled in Rome on 25 July 1943, and six weeks later, on 8 September, the Italians surrender entirely, having been chased off the island of Sicily like dogs by the British and Americans during Operation Husky. Yet once again, that is just the start of the drama. For while the Brits and Americans have beaten the Italians, the Germans now want the Italians to give in as well – in Greece. In any case, they want the history books to not only say the Italians 'surrendered to the Brits and Americans'. And would you believe it – it works. Or at least it looks like it will…

The Italians press their uniforms, polish their shoes and wait for the Germans to come along. And along they come, surprised at how easy it all is. In northern Greece, the 1,000-strong 2nd Brandenburg Regiment disarms 14,000 Italians *en bloc* and without firing a single shot, while the Italian navy stationed in the Aegean appears to be grateful for the arrival of the now officially enemy Germans, and not only ignores Rome's orders to sink their own ships but contributes 'through particularly comradely aid' to the Germans' appropriation of 'two destroyers, four torpedo boats, five E-boats, one mine ship, sixteen auxiliary mine-seeking boats, fourteen small auxiliary vehicles, two tank ships, two troop transporters and six freight ships', whereby both sides do their utmost to prevent any Greeks from witnessing the manoeuvre, as the latter, they agree, should only be watching tragedies, not comedies. As a thank you for playing along so nicely, the Italians are allowed to pick five of the 52 surrendered ships at the end and inflict sham damage on them, making it look like they did at least try to put up a fight. No wonder there's soon a rumour going around Greece that a complete Italian unit on the Peloponnese laid down its arms before a single German soldier, who happened to show up and claimed to have lost his way.

On Corfu, in contrast, fronts collide. The 11,000 Italians stationed there don't fancy playing along with the farce, so they open up the big book of history in front of the German negotiator and inform him they only want to surrender to the Brits and Americans, not the Germans, and declare 'the most glorious and tragic page of recent Italian military history is about to be turned.'

What turns up next are the Germans, but their nautical attack of 13 September 1943, launched by 12 confiscated Greek fishing cutters and a series of unrigged assault boats, ends 500 metres off the coast of Corfu with one dead, seven wounded and the loss of the front vessel.

The idea of the sacking by sea is put to rest, and the Luftwaffe takes a turn, only too willing to show what it can do in Greece, and only one day later, on 14 September 1943, the German planes tip tonnes of aerial mines over Corfu Town, blast holes in roofs and throw down fire bombs after them. Corfu burns for 72 hours running.

Yet the air raid on the capital is not enough to capture the island itself, and as the Italians are still putting up resistance, the Wehrmacht commanders soon call in warships and request heavily armed troops to take Corfu.

Lo and behold, after the neighbouring island of Kefalonia is stormed on 21/22 September, with over 5,000 Italian soldiers taken prisoner and massacred by Wehrmacht units in isolated valleys, on 24 September Operation 'Betrayal' begins on Corfu, in the course of which the German troops conquer the island 'with Stuka support' in the space of a few hours, killing 600 Italian soldiers and taking 10,000 prisoners. The enemy is thus, as

Wehrmacht lingo would have it, 'cast off', yet most of the Italians are not murdered as actually planned (and implemented in Kefalonia), but treated as prisoners of war. At least, the rank-and-file soldiers are. The Italian officers are ordered to get in line for execution in order of rank: 'staff officers singly, the other officers in pairs or threes.'

The subsequent trials are extremely brief. The verdicts are announced, the officers shot 'in a dignified manner' and their corpses submerged in the sea. The sea, knowing no dignity, washes them back up on nearby beaches a few days later.

The rest of the former island-occupying force, the 10,000 captured Italian soldiers, have meanwhile been taken to the airport by Wehrmacht units and shoved into barracks and sheds. Denying food to the men kept in such cramped conditions is part of it. The complete lack of toilet facilities likewise. That the Americans want to join in the big ball game of the cultured nations only becomes clear to the Italians later.

On 4 October, American P-38 bombers attack Corfu airport. No one can say how many Italian soldiers lose their lives in the attack, as only some of them are wiped out from above, whereas others are shot by German ground troops while 'attempting escape'. Five days later, the survivors are loaded onto the *Mario Roselli*, a 140-metre-long steel colossus tasked with taking the mass of Italian prisoners to the Greek mainland, whereby the German soldiers are ordered to 'utilise the transport space up to the utmost limits, regardless of all concerns'.

The British bombers have no concerns either. It's a big game after all, and no cultured nation wants to be left out. On the morning of 10 October, they fly to Corfu in place of their American colleagues and attack the *Mario Roselli* just under a kilometre off the coast. The ship is severely damaged by numerous hits, develops a heavy list and threatens to go under. Most of the Italian soldiers jump overboard. Many of them drown. Those who make it back to land are taken back to the airport barracks. Those who stay put spend the night on a sinking ship. The next morning they're all in for it again, the only difference being that now, on 11 October 1943, British *and* American bomber planes approach the island, attack the airport and sink the *Mario Roselli* once and for all.

The outcome:
Dead Italians: 1302.
Sham damage: none.

For the Italians, that's the end of the drama. For the residents of Corfu, however, it continues, beginning anew on this day, as barely has the *Mario Roselli* been seen to when a few of the Allied bombers branch off to the south and fire on a number of villages where Greeks are queuing on the streets for leftover vegetables to stave off the approaching winter of starvation. Three hundred of them die. The nearby German mountain infantry, who have captured the island, are not attacked.

Shortly after that, the mountain troops leave Corfu, and Hasso Grabner is washed up on the island with his penal battalion. The unworthy men were actually supposed to fight and 'prove themselves in brave and courageous deployment against the enemy'. But then the Wehrmacht didn't quite dare to deploy them in an operation by the name of 'Betrayal'. The German commanders know: 'You can't fight a battle with this cluster of several thousand *Untermenschen*.' Not even against Italians.

The staff commanders would have liked to do just that: appointed the treacherous 999th battalion as the main landing group in the assault on Corfu, loaded them onto boats and sent them over to the similarly treacherous Italians. And then purge, purge, purge: the island, of Italians. Who are now dead with dirty shoes.

Yes, that would have been just the trick, if the treacherous Germans and the treacherous Italians had shot each other up. Unfortunately though, Corfu is too strategically significant for the Wehrmacht to risk staging a comedy of that kind and laughing themselves to death in the process.

But the German commanders do have their fun on Corfu nonetheless, their logic being as flagellant as it is flexible. The withdrawal of the mountain infantry was just as planned as the post-slaughter deployment of Hasso Grabner's penal battalion, for one thing is absolutely clear to the Wehrmacht commanders: if the Allies attack, they can't hold Corfu anyway. So they kill two birds with one stone: fetch the mountain troops off the island and send on the penal soldiers as cannon fodder.

And where's the punchline? Here it comes: until the Allies stationed across the Adriatic attack Corfu (*if* they even do), the commanders condemn the unworthy men to prove themselves on the malaria front; the wretched mosquitos in large parts of Greece including Corfu being a genuine plague. In some battalions, almost half the soldiers fall ill with malaria, and although it's not the fatal tropical version, the consequences are nothing that should be imposed on a healthy member of the master race. At least not as long as there are plenty of communist *Untermenschen* to be had. And if they don't pop their clogs or – the other possibility – get popped off by the invading Allies, at least there's something to laugh at: 'There was one who jumped around in his delirium like a dog and barked. Another leapt at an officer and tried to strangle him.'

And Hasso Grabner? He gets lucky twice over; his deployment on the malaria front is not planned until later – and will go very differently to the Wehrmacht's plans. For the time being, however, Grabner is released from his penal company and sent to the north of Corfu as a battalion radio operator, in a village called Karousades where he doesn't have much to do, what with the situation now being absolutely quiet, according to the Wehrmacht reports, seeing as the Italians are dead or shipped away and the local Greeks apparently deeply relaxed. 'The population is quiet and correct towards the German Wehrmacht, largely even friendly.'

No wonder Hasso Grabner soon seeks out the local beach, lies down in the scrubby marram grass and associates the green and brown objects flying across his field of vision with anything but British planes. What's flying above the beach at Karousades really isn't bomber planes, but an armada of thistle fluff blown up by the wind, which is just as much part of the local climate as the fact that it's briskly cold in Karousades in the autumn of '43, for which reason Hasso Grabner prefers to spend the evenings in his castle.

The impressive old pile in which the battalion radio operator Hasso Grabner not only works but also lives dates back to the 16th century and not long ago belonged to a count by the name of Kōnstantínos Theotókīs. Theotókīs himself had studied in Germany at the end of the 19th century and come into contact with socialist ideas there, ideas he had internalised to such an extent by the time he completed his studies that he not only propagated them on his return to Corfu, but also attempted to put them into practice for himself, which led to him rejecting the inheritance of his highly influential aristocratic family and – rather than becoming an archbishop, prime minister or at least a member of parliament like his brothers, nephews, uncles and various ancestors – founding a socialist trade union federation on Corfu and writing a series of novels, all of them focused on the class struggle.

It is as though the two biographies were mirror images reflected in that castle, in the year 1943. Theotókīs, deceased for 20 years, came from Corfu, went to Germany and came across socialism there, only to return and attempt to spread its teachings, writing under its auspices.

Twenty years later, Hasso Grabner, who came from Germany and went to Corfu, was also to be part of a socialist movement and write novels no less concerned with the class struggle. At this point, however, he knows nothing of all that. At this point he's still stuck in Corfu. In a castle. And Germany, indeed even the war, seems infinitely far away.

And yet it is still there. And Hasso Grabner, the communist in Wehrmacht uniform, is a part of it. But what can he do?

Two thousand kilometres away from Corfu, the illegal leadership committee of the Communist Party of Germany, imprisoned in the Brandenburg house of correction, knows the answer to that question. At least with regard to the communists among the members of the 999th Penal Division. The committee recommends that they use every opportunity to defect – 'to the Soviet troops, or to the partisans in Greece.'

People behind bars sometimes have difficulties imagining mobility. But when they do envisage it, it's all very easy. All you have to do is run off and you'll be with the Soviet troops or the partisans in a jiffy. Except, sadly, there are no partisans in Corfu. Even the German secret service reports: 'Organised bandit activity non-existent from either communist or EDES side.'

'But the Soviet troops! Defect to the Soviet troops!' the KPD leaders proclaim from their 2000-kilometre distance. Only there are not only no partisans, but also no Soviet troops on Corfu. Indeed, the Russians couldn't give a flying Fury about Greece as a whole. One thing's for sure: Stalin's emissaries send millions of warm words to the communist resistance fighters during the war, but not a single cold bullet.

And Stalin himself? He meets up with Churchill and watches him spontaneously sketch out his idea for the future division of the Balkans 'on a half-sheet of paper'. On the subject of Greece, Churchill's suggestion is as follows: Britain 90 %, Russia 10 %.

'I pushed this across to Stalin. There was a slight pause. Then he took his blue pencil and made a large tick upon it, and passed it back to us.'

Two thousand kilometres west of Moscow, in Brandenburg, the imprisoned KPD leadership knows nothing of this deal and continues to persistently demand that its men defect to the Soviet troops or the partisans in Greece. Hasso Grabner, meanwhile, sits in his castle, notes down the incoming Wehrmacht radio dispatches and uses them to build his own kaleidoscope of the island.

Eight years later, by which time most of the images have faded and a new resumé forces his memories into the Procrustean bed of the next ideology, one of them is still very much present. Back-translated into words, it reads: 'In 1943, I was sent to the island of Corfu. There was no active resistance movement there, no partisans.'

And even if there had been: when you defect on an island, you're still stuck on an island.

All around Corfu, meanwhile, the war continues; only on the island, so it seems, is nothing happening. Although the Allied troops are only a 20-minute flight away, controlling the entire airspace above the Adriatic and dropping the occasional bomb on Corfu, most of the time the island is in a strange state of calm, and it almost appears as though Corfu is a prisoner-of-war camp 'in which the Germans manage and take care of themselves.'

In the spring of '44, however, conditions begin to shift. The pre-stabilised harmony of the uncontested coexistence with the Allied troops stationed in Italy starts to slip almost without a sound. And the Albanian partisans, too, raise their heads from their hiding places and peer across at Corfu. Well, I never. Things really are happening on the island…

In May '44, a British plane lands in the south of Corfu. This part of the island being largely unoccupied by the Germans, a Wehrmacht reconnaissance troop is immediately dispatched. By the time they arrive, however, they can only report that the plane has burnt out and the crew vanished.

On the rocky island of Othonoi, considered the key to the Adriatic due to its exposed position northwest of Corfu, unknown parties mount an attack on a Wehrmacht base in July '44. The German staff, headquartered 25 kilometres away in Karousades, experiences the assault at almost first hand. The uncapped radio connection broadcasts the sound of hand-grenade explosions and screams live. Partisans are suspected, but the attackers are never caught.

A few days later, a British submarine is reported to have appeared in the bay of Sidari on the west coast of Corfu. The observers cannot say whether anyone disembarked, as the guards are poorly distributed. Nevertheless: 'The impression is increasingly prevalent that Corfu is forming a base for the Allies to infiltrate the south-eastern area with agents, to support the mainland partisans.'

Shortly after that, flashing lights and signals are sighted on the sea off Corfu and on the opposite Albanian mainland. German counterintelligence attempt to identify the signals but are soon forced to admit that the messages' senders and receivers are not only unknown, but also remain invisible. One thing has been visible from the outset, however: the Jews on the island.

It is April 1944, and the Corfiot Jews feel safe, despite the German occupation. Their community is one of the oldest in Greece, their significance for the island's economic survival is undisputed, and their protection is ensured by a Red Cross ship moored in the harbour. At some point this month, the radio operator Hasso Grabner receives from his superior in Karousades castle a confidential, doubly coded command document. The writ orders the company command posts on the island to report all Jewish residents in their catchment areas.

Over the subsequent 48 hours, all of the 2000 Jews living in Corfu are placed on lists and forced to present themselves regularly to the German authorities from then on. The attendant humiliations are tacitly accepted, and no protest is raised. On the contrary, the president of Corfu's Jewish religious community calls on its members to follow the Germans' instructions. They have nothing to fear, he tells them.

Hasso Grabner, meanwhile, attempts to use all channels available to him in Karousades castle. He knows what this census signifies, and he succeeds in warning one Jewish man who lives in the village. He manages no more than that. He, the middleman who recently helped to enable the night landing of a British submarine, seems absolutely helpless on the Jewish question.

On 25 April, the head of the relevant German department declares there are 'no fundamental concerns' with regard to the deportation of Corfu's Jews and that sufficient shipping capacity is available.

On 12 May, the German police department in Athens informs Army Group E, stationed on Corfu, that the removal of the Jews is imminent and should be performed 'at accelerated speed'. The legal basis, they add, is an order by SS-Reichsführer Himmler.

On 14 May, SS-Obersturmführer Anton Burger, newly arrived on the island and in charge of Jewish affairs, orders the island commandant Emil Jäger to arrest all Jews on Corfu without delay. The island commandant, however, intervenes.

Jäger, the owner of a riding hall in civilian life, is actually a loyal servant to the Führer, so loyal that he kept a seat free for him at all party events under his own organisation for years, and at some point – since the Führer never showed his face – undertook to speak to him directly, albeit not in person but in written form, which he entitled 'A Fateful Contribution from the NSDAP's Time of Struggle in Austria' and sent to Hitler's confidant Martin Bormann, with a request to present his opus to the Führer.

Now, however, as island commandant of Corfu, Jäger does not want to have 'his' Jews simply arrested, let alone deported; after all, he explains, the Red Cross ship is still in the harbour and would 'ensure propaganda of atrocities'. Aside from that, he adds, the local population sides with the Jews, meaning 'the inevitable brutality can only have a repellent effect'. The consequences: 'loss of ethical prestige' and 'moral damage to the troops' – not the only price to be paid, however, as the Jews, according to Jäger, possess 'considerable amounts of gold, jewels, fabrics' and other items that would 'corrupt our soldiers and the German authority in the form of bribes' and 'only aid the enemy to a great extent'. He suggests that the army commanders therefore 'postpone for the foreseeable future'.

In Karousades castle, Hasso Grabner can't quite believe his ears. Not only does it look like the Jews won't be deported after all; no, if he is to believe the island commandant's words, they have also been warned. The helplessness he felt only days ago vanishes into thin air.

It is dangerous for Grabner to display his joy at the developments openly, but he does want to express it. Over the next few days he writes a series of poems, a kind of Corfiot trilogy of fulfilment, leading – by means of a massive poetic analogy – from night to dawn to the brightness of day. The opening lines of the last verse, written on 28 May 1944, are: 'Joyous sky of Corfu, your sounds / echo from the gentle mounts.'

Five days later, it's the sonorous tone of Allied bomber planes echoing from the island's mountains, as the British and Americans undertake another air raid on Corfu. The bombs they drop are real, the buildings they land on are reduced to rubble and the people they hit are as dead as only bombs can kill. And yet the attack is purely for decorative purposes, intended only to distract attention from the Allied landings in Normandy.

On the ground in Corfu, however, the German army command is creating cold hard facts. On the evening of 8 June 1944, the island's Jews are instructed to gather in the town the next day, while Hasso Grabner and all the penal-battalion soldiers receive orders to keep out of what is to happen tomorrow.

On 9 June, the Corfiot Jews become the victims of the largest raid in the island's history. Only few of them try to escape to the mountains, with many Jews even placing themselves directly in the Germans' hands. It is not easy to say why. Perhaps they are in a similar situation to the communists in Wehrmacht uniform, perhaps they simply don't believe they might find safe harbour on an island. More likely, however, the Jews of Corfu trust in their history and their importance to the economy – and trust even more in the high-ranking members of their religious community, who cannot imagine their own extermination. It is not the first time that the credulous become corpses. A year previously, the president of Thessaloniki's Jewish community warned the Jews threatened with deportation against fleeing, saying that it would displease the Germans, and that the new settlement area in Poland appeared promising. Most of the more than 40,000 Jews of Thessaloniki believed him. Only few of them fled their homes. Those who remained were arrested and deported to Auschwitz and Treblinka, where three quarters of them were gassed. Did they know that the president of the community had once written his PhD thesis in Vienna, on descriptions of hell in Jewish literature?

In Corfu, meanwhile, almost 1700 Jews have gathered outside the town's old fortress at six o'clock in the morning of 9 June 1944. Those who don't turn up voluntarily are beaten out of their homes; patients in hospitals and asylums are promptly 'released'.

The people milling around outside the fortress aren't the only ones up and about that morning. On balconies, behind windows encased in thick walls, on top of roofs and houses, everywhere groups of people whisper and watch as the Corfiot Jews below them form a great group, an island on the island, penned in by Wehrmacht, Gestapo and Greek police officers, who wear no uniforms. The Rikanati brothers, Jews from Athens, also help the Germans.

And so it proceeds. The Corfiot Jews are sorted, searched and then robbed of their belongings. Even their house keys are taken from them. And the Red Cross ship has also departed.

Other ships have come in its place, and while the Jews wait in Corfu's old fortress for their fate to unfold, and every thought of escape ends in the barrel of a German machine gun, Wehrmacht-chartered boats are preparing for their load in the city's harbour, and two days later, on 11 June 1944, the deportation begins.

Since there is neither food nor water on the crossing, the number of living passengers is reduced by several dozen on the way to Patras via Lefkada. That is essentially in the Germans' interest, however. The question of disposal was clarified nine months previously by the example of the Italian army officers; the problem of washed-up corpses is discussed, and a promise is given that it will not happen again. The dead are therefore weighed down before they are thrown in the sea, and the fact that they do not get washed up on the beaches is taken as proof that the Wehrmacht has learned from its mistakes.

Once the shipping is done, the Corfiot Jews are interned in the Haidari concentration camp near Athens before being taken to Auschwitz in cattle cars. The rail journey takes nine days. Many of them die of starvation or thirst. When the Jews arrive in Auschwitz on the evening of 29 June, most of them are immediately murdered and burned in crematorium number two.

And on Corfu? The beaches are clean as a whistle, and the Greek mayor holds a party in mid-July. 'Our good friends the Germans have cleansed the island of the Jewish vermin. Now we must no longer share the harvests of our fields with them.'

Two weeks later, the war in Corfu has finally degenerated to the grotesque; from now on, a British fighter plane circles the island every morning. It is not attacked, but nor does it attack anything or anyone itself, and it almost appears as though the Italians and Jews had been its preferred targets. The German soldiers, at any rate, soon grow accustomed to this exquisitely English form of encirclement, watching the plane fly its relentless loops of the island, at some point calling it 'the duty officer from the other side'.

And yet the thing with the 'other side' is not quite as simple and peaceful as it seems; to be precise, there are two other sides on Corfu. And while one of them comes from outside, belongs to the Royal Air Force and offers aerial tours around Corfu every morning, the other is stationed on the island itself: loyal members of the KPD despite their Wehrmacht uniforms, who spend every free hour building a model of their own base out of matchsticks.

What may sound like a pointless creative exercise actually has a political motivation. For months, the soldiers' newspaper *Wacht im Südosten* has been tub-thumping for the special exhibition 'Combat Area Southeast' to be mounted 'in the near future in Vienna', even offering a prize for the best model of a Wehrmacht base.

There can be no better cover story. The communists in Hasso Grabner's penal battalion take up firstly the challenge, secondly the opportunity to meet regularly on an absolutely unsuspicious pretext, and consequently, thirdly, they take the matter appropriately seriously, so it is no wonder that they end up – tadaaa! – winning the thing.

The man who awards the prize to the soldiers, all allegedly acting out of personal motivation and enjoyment of fascist propaganda, is Wilhelm Hammer, a counterintelligence officer in Army Group E. He has no idea that the prize-winners are communists whose real mission is planning a coup on Corfu, not making matchstick models.

There really are plans to take the island back from the Wehrmacht – and Hasso Grabner is in the midst of them, the node of a web of information which runs from his radio station in Karousades castle via the company command posts to the remotest of grenade launcher positions.

But German counterintelligence on Corfu is not inactive, and soon requests secret military police, standard military police and additional counterintelligence troops 'for the surveillance of unreliable elements of the local battalion of unworthy men'.

Meanwhile, a few kilometres from Karousades, the penal soldier Hans Binder has made contact with Greek resistance fighters. Binder, whose story is lost in an obscure gloom of rumours and half-truths, and whose political views veer somewhere between communist, cryptic and criminal, soon lets his direct associate Hasso Grabner in on his plans.

Grabner, however, is sceptical. With his connection to the staff commanders and his position providing him with wide-ranging information, he warns against hasty actions. Under the conditions of an island, and Corfu only harbouring few hidden partisans while the Wehrmacht is well established, he considers direct actions against the German occupiers far too dangerous.

Hans Binder does not want to hear about risks and dangers; Hans Binder wants to do something. So he tries to win over other penal soldiers for his plans, not excluding the 'criminals' in the 999th Division – who end up betraying him.

On the evening of 8 September 1944, German counterintelligence men raid the house Binder uses as an illicit meeting place and arrest the Greek partisans they find inside. Binder, on duty that evening and not present, is dragged out of a rifle pit shortly later, taken to a nearby police prison and 'questioned' by the secret military police. During the simultaneous search of his belongings, they find a small notebook containing the names of those he has informed of his plans. Hasso Grabner's name is at the very top of the list.

That same night, Grabner receives a visit at Karousades castle from three Wehrmacht soldiers, who command him to come with them. He does not know what he is accused of. Nor does he know where he's going, and not until the end of a three-hour march taking him to the western part of the island, to the picturesque village of Paleokastriza, does Hasso Grabner know what awaits him. Tied to an olive tree in the rising morning light, he finds Hans Binder.

Grabner immediately sees that the military police have prepared Binder for execution. His hands are tied behind his back and his eyes are covered. All that is merely decorative, though; Hans Binder cannot see a thing any more. His face has been beaten to a pulp, his left eye socket now completely empty.

Hasso Grabner is soon likewise shackled and tied to a post only metres away from Hans Binder, but the men purposely leave his eyes uncovered. He is to watch his comrade dying.

Shortly afterwards, Hasso Grabner hears the familiar command and sees the firing squad's bullets hit the shackled body. Yet they don't kill Hans Binder. Instead, the commanding officer steps forward, stands directly in front of Binder hanging from the tree, and looks at Grabner as if to challenge him. When he sees that Grabner is watching, he takes his gun and shoots Hans Binder in the face, not once taking his eyes off Grabner. The tied-up body crumples.

That is the last thing Hasso Grabner sees. Then his eyes, too, are covered and the command rings out. 'Aim. Fire!'

Not a shot is heard, only howls of laughter. After a while, Grabner is untied. 'It'll be serious next time, you communist swine,' the officer tells him, clearly looking forward to it. Then the three soldiers take Hasso Grabner back to Karousades.

Essentially, the Wehrmacht on Corfu in 1944 is in the same position as the judge nine years previously in Dresden. They think they've taught Hasso Grabner a lesson, but he's long since learned his own. When he finds out the next day, through the radio troop commander stationed with him in the castle, that, as a result of Binder's treason, the entire penal battalion on the island is to be disarmed and every tenth soldier to be shot, he immediately passes the news on to the 'political' penal soldiers serving with him, and with good luck and diplomatic skills, they manage to thwart the plan. Hasso Grabner breathes a sigh of relief when he hears over the radio that the order to disarm has been reversed and the planned executions have also been called off. A few days later, however, his chest constricts again.

It is late September, and Hasso Grabner finds out via a series of top-secret channels that the local administrator of Karousades, Konstantinos Kladas, has spoken in favour of making him, the communist in Wehrmacht uniform, an honorary citizen. His reasoning is that Grabner, whom everyone in the village simply calls 'the doctor', has rendered outstanding services to the village by relieving the Wehrmacht antimalarial stocks of 10,000 Atebrin tablets and giving them to the local people – something everyone knows but no one says out loud. He has also 'reallocated' German guards on several occasions via radio, thereby enabling the landing of a boatful of resistance fighters from Albania, and done everything he could to come into contact with the Greeks and their resistance fighters.

But Hasso Grabner doesn't want to be an honorary citizen of Karousades. Hasso Grabner wants to go home.

A few days later, he gets a chance to do so. On 1 October 1944, the Germans pull out of Corfu. Shortly before that, the entire 999th battalion has been swiftly declared worthy of military service after all, and every private has been made a private first class. The only exception from this mass promotion is Hasso Grabner. The army commanders are not reckoning on him surviving anyway. His unit is the last in the west wing of Army Group E. And the rear guard on a retreat is always the first to feel the enemy's attack. The losses, the commanders estimate, will be extremely high.

Cool winds blow from Albania's peaks to the land.
In greeting to Skanderbeg's eagles, I raise a brotherly hand.

Hasso Grabner, 'To the Eagles beyond the Straits of Corfu'
Corfu, 15 April 1944

Heading Home

Essentially, from October '44 there's nothing but friendly fire, all the way across Albania. And Hasso Grabner in its midst.

Grabner, who was just about to be honoured on Corfu for his help landing Albanian partisans from Saranda, is now shot at by partisans from Saranda on 1 October, while landing from Corfu. What makes it almost bearable is the fact that among the Albanian forces that have surrounded the town and opened fire are two Leipzig communists, who have fled from their 999th battalion units and are now fighting alongside the partisans, as instructed by the KPD. The fact that the partisans initially order the 1200 British marines landed north of Saranda to leave – and only let them join in the shooting after a few lessons on how to fire a barrage – leaves room for survival, at least in and around Saranda. Still, 400 Wehrmacht soldiers are left to die. Hasso Grabner is not among them.

What follows is a large S-shaped curve, by which Grabner's battalion moves across Albania. From the south to the east, back to the middle and then across the west of the country to leave it in the north. And all that remains is places with names the soldiers have never heard before (Delvina, Korça, Struga, Elbasan), losses that can only be estimated ('Tirana: approx. 1500 men'), and a tropical uniform that turns Wehrmacht soldiers into the laughing stock of the Albanian mountains.

'The march back,' Hasso Grabner will later report, 'was of inconceivable severity. There could be no thought of defecting. The partisans, particularly the Albanians, took no prisoners.'

Nor, in fact, do they recognise the communists and antifascist resistance fighters among the ranks of the Wehrmacht, and when Hasso Grabner's company is attacked in its camp one night there's no time for explanations. It's a matter of survival. Hasso Grabner shoots his tracer ammunition in the face of one of the fast-approaching partisans and rams his bayonet in the belly of another.

Not until the next morning, once the battle is over and the clearing up is part of the slaughterers' job, does Hasso Grabner see that the man he stabbed has a red star on his hat. He secretly removes it. The pocketed star is his souvenir of what unofficially was a battle between brothers and in the official Wehrmacht parlance was a victory over the enemy, as a result of which Hasso Grabner is awarded the Close Combat Clasp for hand-to-hand fighting.

So there he stands, Hasso Grabner, holding two souvenirs and not knowing which of them is more terrible.

A bow is tied, a knot pulled tight. Ten years ago, Hasso Grabner distributed an illegal newspaper in Leipzig. It was the second edition of *Junge Garde*, and it brought him – via Waldheim, Buchenwald, the Heuberg and Corfu – here to Albania. That newspaper featured an article about communist resistance, with the words: 'We will take up the weapons of the bourgeoisie, yet we will not turn them against our brothers beyond the borders, but aim them at the enemy in our own land.'

Now, beyond those borders, the communist brothers' class struggle falls at the hurdle of outward appearances. Anyone traipsing through the snowy Albanian mountains in the tropical uniform of the German Wehrmacht can only hope, if not for pity, then for a mercy killing.

Eventually, in November 1944, the Fortress Brigade 1017, to which Hasso Grabner's battalion now belongs, is completely kettled by Albanian partisans on the Edelweiss Pass near Tirana and comes under fire. Their attempts to fight back are laughable, and their losses so high that they are soon counting only survivors, burying the corpses in shallow graves in hurriedly constructed cemeteries. The rest is taken care of by the local wolves and the Albanian snow.

Hasso Grabner is one of those who has to dig graves, plant crosses and bury the fallen. He carves a short poem into one of the crosses. No one cares now that the verse is against war. The officers are tired. A few weeks later, Hasso Grabner also gets his cross.

Before that, though, the retreat across the Albanian mountains goes on. Yet the soldiers are soon sinking ever deeper into the snow, lying down and refusing to go on. Hasso Grabner does not want to lie still, though. Hasso Grabner wants to go home. So he cheers up his comrades, drags them upright, drives them onwards. If need be by poking backsides lying prone in the snow with his pocket knife. And when in December 1944 he helps to free several soldiers from his company from a house under attack by partisans, Hasso Grabner finally gets what's coming to him. On 2 January 1945, he is awarded the Iron Cross second class 'in the name of the Führer' for 'bravery in the face of the enemy'.

To Grabner, the medal is terribly embarrassing, but the company leader saves the day in his own way, yelling, 'You see, Grabner, you old communist swine, now you do have to march around with a swastika on your chest after all.'

And Grabner marches. 'Driven by a desire to be in my homeland on its collapse,' he leaves Albania behind him, makes it through Montenegro, crosses the 2500-metre Durmitor Massif – with communist ideals in his head and the Iron Cross on his chest –

and eventually gets to what is at the time the 'Independent State of Croatia'. From here, he knows, it's still well over a thousand kilometres to home.

On 18 January 1945, Hasso Grabner absents himself from his troop in Sarajevo. He is aware he is deserting. But what choice does he have? His battalion has already been decimated by 90 per cent and, as the number of potential victims shrinks, at some point anyone's luck would run out.

What follows is unknown territory, then as now. Hasso Grabner sticks to the north-western course. Written history keeps out of the matter. Not a single source, not one obscure piece of paper provides information on what happens to Hasso Grabner in January and February of '45. The only thing we know for sure is that he arrives in Neunkirchen, Austria, in March and that his arms, hands and legs are littered with shrapnel. When Hasso Grabner holds his left hand up to the light, it looks like tiny fish are swimming across his palm.

Neunkirchen itself is so pretty that Hasso Grabner would like nothing better than to keep going, but the Wehrmacht has set up a field hospital there. The war, it seems, has once again topped up the battalion of potential victims. Now, however, as the matter is nearing an end, all it has left is injured men. Half a dozen barracks are stuffed full of them.

When four American bomber planes approach on the evening of 26 March, Hasso Grabner is in the field hospital's garden. When they leave again, the number of injured men in the barracks has fallen significantly.

On 28 March the worst of the shrapnel is removed from Hasso Grabner's body. The rest stays put. For later. As a reminder of the possibility of war. And the impossibility of erasing its traces.

Hasso Grabner's traces reappear now, the unknown territory behind him. Ahead of him, however, is the bomb-devastated office of the Wehrmacht field hospital. Freshly operated, Hasso Grabner ventures in, finds a piece of paper, grabs a pen – and writes his own discharge certificate. A random rubber stamp confirms the matter, and Hasso Grabner can continue his homeward journey. In Vienna he catches the last train to Leipzig, and on 1 April 1945 he's back in town.

Another soldier from Leipzig, meanwhile, is less lucky, even though he's been in presumed safety since March of '44. In a POW camp in Oklahoma, a fortress infantryman named Kuhnert is condemned as an enemy of the Great German Reich by Wehrmacht soldiers for his involvement in a 999th battalion, and stoned to death with heavy porcelain mugs.

Kuhnert is not the only misfortunate soul to suffer this fate. In the French POW camp Pont du Fass, numerous political 999ers are stomped to death beneath the boots of Wehrmacht soldiers imprisoned alongside them, while the German units held by the Allies in Tunisian Bizerta are so sure of themselves that they call themselves the 'Club of Overstrong Nazi Men' and sentence those they consider 'dishonourable soldiers' to death in a veritable court procedure, post the verdict in the camp and then strangle and hang the 'unworthy men'.

In Leipzig, meanwhile, Hasso Grabner hides out in a hospital run by nuns.

Intermezzo – Leipzig, April '45

1 April 1945 is Easter Sunday, and while a few stragglers embark on egg hunts in the parks of Leipzig, Hasso Grabner has good reason to hide out at a hospital in the west of the city. The Nazis know their end is nigh, and anyone who falls into their hands and makes even the slightest impression of treason gets not even a perfunctory trial, but none whatsoever.

On 12 April, 65 political prisoners previously forced to serve in the Wehrmacht as soldiers are picked up from a Leipzig prison by the Gestapo and sent to Dresden for the purpose of their later liquidation.

On 13 April, concurrent to the Gestapo's physical extermination of its opponents, it instigates a paperwork-killing campaign. One particularly active participant is Paul Budin, the director general of the Leipzig company HASAG, one of the largest armament firms in the German Reich, which of late produced anti-tank grenades for the glorious German victory, with the aid of thousands of Jewish forced labourers. In an effort to destroy as much evidence as possible, Budin blows up the entire HASAG administration building at precisely 23:50 hours. Then he disappears. Whether into the rubble of his company or to another country, no one knows to this day.

On 14 April, the political prisoner Karl Franz is court-martialled and executed by a Wehrmacht firing squad in Leipzig due to his antifascist views. Before that, the Gestapo chartered a bus from a local travel company to drive to two police prisons, collected 53 political prisoners, took them to a parade ground in the north of the city and executed them with bullets to the back of the neck. This time, no graves have to be shovelled because an American air raid two days previously has left behind a sufficiently large bomb crater. Once the last man has tipped over the edge, spitting blood, the Gestapo killers seek out a master butcher who lives nearby, arrest him, confiscate his hams and all the alcohol in the house, and round off the day with a meat-fuelled drinking session.

On 15 April, finally, Hans von Poncet, bearer of the Knight's Cross and newly appointed combat commandant of Leipzig, takes up his command post inside the monument to the 1813 Battle of the Nations, a 300,000-tonne, 90-metre castle of tamped concrete and granite, 'with a gesture of determination to fight'. Meanwhile, the city's natural history museum doesn't let that stop it from holding a guided bird-spotting tour of the directly adjacent South Cemetery.

Thirty years later, Hasso Grabner will be standing on that same monument, looking down at that South Cemetery and informing his wife that this is the place where he would like to be laid to rest. He still has plenty of time until then, though. And no rest, although he is now condemned, on this 15 April 1945, to do nothing but rest, lying in a goddamn hospital and not knowing whether he'll be discovered and if so, by whom. To say nothing of the question of what would happen then.

On 16 April, Leipzig's first tank alarm rings. At the South Cemetery, the burials for the day are postponed because no one can be found to dig the graves. Aside from that, it's a nice day. The first daffodils are blossoming in Leipzig's parks.

On 17 April, a new warning sound is heard in Leipzig: enemy alarm! The Americans have reached the city. Many of them are Black. They use unfamiliar ultrashort-wave walkie-talkies.

On 18 April, at around 12:30 hours, 300 prisoners are locked into a barracks shed in a Leipzig sub-camp of Buchenwald concentration camp, the windows and doors are nailed shut and hundreds of litres of petrol are poured over the building. A dozen SS men and Volkssturm* militia recruits then set it alight. Those who attempt to escape the flames are shot down with anti-tank grenades and machine guns. At 20:00 hours, the murderers call the local Gestapo to pick them up and drive them home. In New Town Hall, Leipzig's city fathers are meanwhile preparing for their last great performance.

On 19 April, American soldiers find the mayor in his office. He is sitting in a circle with his wife and daughter, while in the next room the city treasurer holds his head in his hands, his wife leaning back in an armchair opposite and their daughter reclining on a sofa. A bottle of Pyrimal, clearly visible on the desk, reveals the sleepers to be corpses, and the documents carefully arranged beside the medication help identify the dead.

In the catacombs of the Battle of the Nations monument, however, there is to be no talk of surrender, even though 155-mm grenades are being fired at the monument by the minute and every shot is a direct hit. Yet the missiles that hit the walls bounce right off, and what splinters off is ridiculously small in comparison to the monument, the boulders flying through the air more of a danger to the surrounding houses than to the German occupants inside, who don't let the Allied fire stop them from showing captured American soldiers the valuable books in the crypt and explaining the story of the Battle of the Nations. And indeed, why not? It's the best opportunity they'll ever have to give these American philistines an idea of what a cultured nation Germany is.

Finally, on 20 April, the Leipzig combat commandant surrenders after the American officer negotiating with him quotes a passage from a Kleist play. The assurance the commandant won't be treated as a prisoner of war and will be granted safe passage out of the city makes the decision easier for him. As usual, the German soldiers taken prisoner after the monument's abandonment are not asked for their opinion on the matter – and the fallen American soldiers have no chance to object.

Hasso Grabner, meanwhile, has discharged himself from another hospital.

Every step of real movement is more important than a dozen programmes.

Karl Marx, letter to Wilhelm Bracke, 5 May 1875

At Home

Although American soldiers officially take the Wehrmacht member Hasso Grabner prisoner in a Leipzig convent hospital on 18 April 1945, the prisoner soon manages to escape, upon which the department doctor can only comment: 'Patient left the field hospital without permission and has not returned.'

Before that, however, Hasso Grabner writes himself another kind of discharge certificate; this time not on a random sheet of paper but an American form, on which he enters the appropriate answers. Penal battalion. Absented from the troop. Deserted.

Grabner doesn't mention that he's a communist. The Americans, he thinks, will soon notice that anyway. And in actual fact, by the time the commander-in-chief of the American military government in Leipzig, Major Richard Eaton, bans the antifascist National Committee Free Germany* on 28 April 1945, Hasso Grabner is of course active in precisely that organisation. But that's not a problem for Grabner, quite the opposite; the education-hungry Marxist in him has spent long enough on dialectics to know that prohibitions per se are extremely odd creations, as they impose punishment on satisfying a wish they themselves may have generated in the first place. Be that as it may, Hasso Grabner takes the ban as inspiration to set up a National Committee youth group in May, and to hold an equally illegal conference in June, attended by 300 participants.

Elsewhere in Leipzig, too, the communist will to rebuild is combined with resistance grown in secret for years, prompting the American counterespionage service to radio home on 15 May that they are facing, in the city, 'a German underground movement of size and weight for the first time in the German campaign'.

Hasso Grabner would certainly not deny that. On the contrary; it is as if he had to catch up on the undone political work of the past 11 years in the space of weeks, as though now that the Americans are in town and the Russians just outside it, the moment for the revolution has finally arrived. And so he races across town on his bicycle from morning to night, his thin legs shooting up and down beneath him like the needles of two sewing machines as he unceasingly seams all kinds of plans in his mind, even when he stands still for a moment. But that's rarely the case, and in fact Hasso Grabner loves to do everything at the same time: he jacks through all trades, holds speeches, organises meetings, gets himself a typewriter, bangs out agitprop articles, composes poems on the side, writes a youth anthem and, all that not being enough for him, in August 1945 becomes head of the cultural section of the city's antifascist youth commission. Three weeks later, he takes over as chairman of the entire organisation.

It is the only one that the new, that is, now *Soviet* military administration allows young people to join. The board consists – as does that of the Antifascist Bloc founded at the end of May and also chaired by Grabner – of communists plus social democrats, liberals, non-affiliated individuals and Christians. That is politically reasonable, democratically just and also representative of Leipzig's population, but Walter Ulbricht*'s KPD Initiative Group, just returned from Moscow exile, doesn't like it one bit. Until they finally cement their own power, they want to hear nothing of self-administered initiatives or cross-party blocs, and have no interest in any kind of 'messing around with the antifa'.

Leipzig's communists are brought into line as early as the summer of '45, the Antifascist Bloc brought into the cadre-headed form preferred by the Berlin comrades, and all the remaining committees are, as Ulbricht puts it, 'liquidated'. Anyone who resists and disregards the central perspective in the popular painting of future pictures, is put into the next best prison to scratch matchstick men on the walls.

Hasso Grabner, meanwhile, sticks it out, continues his youth work, joins the Leipzig KPD's district committee, joins the Socialist Unity Party (SED), freshly cemented out of SPD and KPD in April '46, immediately takes up a post on that party's district council and, seeing as the unity party wants to see the youth united as well (and multiple burdens are a matter of course for Grabner the workhorse), is also chairman of Leipzig's newly founded Free Democratic Youth* (FDJ) by March. Or not, as the case may be.

The respective sources disagree on the matter. 'Hasso Grabner becomes FDJ chairman,' it says in one, while another stubbornly insists: 'Alfred Nothnagel takes on chair of Leipzig FDJ.'

Whether Nothnagel, true to his name, is merely a stopgap or really does nail it for the Free German Youth, is ultimately unknowable, but it is not essential for us to know, because it's clear that Hasso Grabner gives up his youth work only a few days after the FDJ is founded, or perhaps has to give it up, as: 'The party posted me to Dresden.'

As everyone knows, for Leipzigers, a posting to nearby Dresden is always a disciplinary measure.

When Grabner arrives in Dresden, he might have a job but he doesn't have a clue; the party has appointed him, a trained bookseller, the director of Central German Broadcasting.

So there he is, Hasso Grabner, in a gigantic ruin by the name of Dresden, with not the slightest clue what to do – and no magnifying glass to find one either. What is to be done?

Hasso Grabner simply doesn't know. But just sitting around and waiting for something to happen has never been his thing. So off he goes. He wanders the streets of the gigantic ruin like a hawker. And begs for everything but bread. 'Excuse me, I'm from the state broadcaster, might you perhaps have a violin?'

Of course, no one has a violin, and if they do then it's not in one piece. But Hasso Grabner the broadcasting director wouldn't be Hasso Grabner the bookseller if he didn't find something else in the dregs of Dresden. French literature, for instance. When he plans to make a radio programme with one of the books he dredges up – Alphonse Daudet's *Tartarin de Tarascon* – the responsible Soviet occupation officer intervenes on the grounds that he doesn't know anything about French literature. Grabner, however, having been gifted by Mother Nature and Father History with a sense of confidence bordering on arrogance, makes the programme anyway. Since the officer likes the result, he's allowed to go on with it. Since the residents of Dresden have other problems than literature, though, he's not allowed to overdo it.

But Hasso Grabner the broadcasting director wouldn't be Hasso Grabner the pragmatist if he didn't make *one* virtue out of two necessities. That is to say, the bombed-out Dresdeners are invited to bring their broken radios into the station, the in-house technicians solve their reception problems, and the satisfied customers are requested to pay their bill live on the spot (thus adding a local element to the schedule). 'Mrs Maria Paudler,' for example, 'sang into the microphone in return for the repair of her radio.'

No wonder Hasso Grabner noted with pride, in retrospect: 'I made the cheapest radio programming in the world, with one Magnetophon tape; when it ran out we had to start chatting.'

And Hasso Grabner is always chatting. Though not for long.

Seeing as he fails to discuss every programme in advance with the censorship authority and occasionally interprets its rulings rather freely, he soon becomes subject to Soviet attention. He doesn't exactly improve matters by turning down the official functionary apartment offered to him in an area guarded by soldiers, on the grounds that he was locked away for long enough. Hasso Grabner appears more and more suspect to the Russians – and his drive for freedom soon becomes a problem. Finally, in May '46, the Soviet military administration has had enough of the director's wayward ideas, demands his removal and declares, with the bewilderment of an authority designed around subordination and submission: 'Hasso Grabner frequently weighs into radio broadcasts – as a reporter!'

Hasso Grabner's career at Central German Broadcasting is over after precisely 49 days.

So there he is in Dresden, in the dregs of the gigantic ruin, not out of ideas but out of a job, while one of his old pals in Leipzig has so much work he doesn't know where to start. His name is Fritz Selbmann, and just like Hasso Grabner he spent the years 1935 to 1938 in the Waldheim house of correction. Perhaps this is the moment when Selbmann, Saxony's Economics and Planning Minister, remembers his old friend Hasso Grabner, or perhaps it's just one of history's usual volte-faces, a small magic trick in the space-time continuum known as history, in the course of which Fritz Selbmann – in a grey loden suit with a mandarin collar and boots with shafts as high as towers – is abruptly teleported back to Waldheim.

'In the mid-1930s,' history explains, as if the minister didn't know so himself, 'countless communists came here.' And then, in that oracular tone so beloved by fortune tellers: 'They came here even though they didn't want to come here, and now, 10 years later, they can't get away from here even though they're long gone.'

'What's that supposed to mean?' Fritz Selbmann might well ask, but he doesn't. Instead, he stands there in Waldheim, outside the house of correction, in his grey loden suit and his boots as high as towers. He looks like a character in a Karl May novel, out of place and oddly dressed. But that doesn't bother Fritz Selbmann, the old KPD ruffian, not in the slightest. He prefers to look eastwards, to the wilds of Dresden, where the raging reporter Hasso Grabner is standing directionless by the side of the road, his head hanging low.

'All you have to do is reach out,' history says – and Fritz Selbmann the trained miner reaches out. He raises his mighty left arm, extends his huge hand – as easy as pie – from Waldheim directly to Dresden, and grabs Hasso Grabner out of there.

Then he pulls him back, switches hands – somewhere in the valley above Waldheim – folds out his right arm to the west, to Leipzig, drops Hasso Grabner down there – and says not a word.

'From now on, you're Fritz's right-hand man,' says history, 'detached for the surveillance of implementation of SMAD commands 124 and 126.'

'The confiscation of Nazi assets?' asks Hasso Grabner, still slightly confused by the sudden relocation.

'That's right, Nazi assets,' says history, 'confiscation, sequestration, expropation.'

'Expropriation,' Hasso Grabner corrects. 'I didn't learn Latin in Waldheim for nothing.'

History says not a word.
Hasso Grabner sets off.
Fritz Selbmann is pleased.
A month later, it's all over again.

Through a referendum, the state of Saxony accepts the 'Law on the surrender of companies owned by war criminals and Nazi criminals into public property' on 30 June 1946. The expropriation of the expropriators has thereby officially begun – and Moscow sends congratulations via traditional clandestine channels. What the Saxon communists have achieved in the briefest of periods, the message reads, is 'the unfurling of a great class struggle in Saxony and beyond that the unfurling of a class struggle in the Soviet zone and further in Germany, indeed the unfurling of a class struggle on a worldwide scale.'

And Hasso Grabner? He continues the worldwide class struggle from the 'Saxon state government, Leipzig sub-office', where he helps to clarify all the decidedly political issues arising in the construction of a publicly owned industrial sector, becoming first an advisor, then a councillor, and finally a senior councillor.

In June of 1948 comes the next stage of the revolution. In the Soviet-occupied zone, the publicly owned companies in each individual branch of industry are combined into economic units. There are to be ten such federations of publicly-owned companies – and the party tasks Hasso Grabner with finding an appropriate director for each of them.

He finds nine, with only number ten showing no sign of turning up. But because what may not be cannot be allowed to happen, the party turns around and makes a recruit out of the recruiter – and on 23 June 1948, Hasso Grabner the trained bookseller, a man who's never seen the inside of a steelworks, is appointed 'Main Director of the Federation for the Production and Processing of Crude Iron, Steel and Rolling-Mill Products', responsible from that point on for the entire East German iron and steel industry.

So there he is in Leipzig, suddenly in charge of two dozen companies with a total of 38,000 employees who produce goods worth billions. Essentially, it's like the retreat from Greece: the whole thing can only go wrong. And if not, it'll rain honours, medals and awards.

On 16 November 1948, Hasso Grabner is the first man outside the mining industry to be awarded the title of 'Activist' by the German Economic Commission, then becomes a 'Citizen of Merit' of the city of Leipzig, and is finally nominated for the National Prize of the GDR. As main director, he's categorized as an 'administration person', so seven of his employees are honoured in his place; that's no big deal though because Grabner is nominated again in 1951. The decision has already been wrapped up internally when the SED Central Committee suddenly and hurriedly asks Grabner to step back from his nomination, 'because a professor who has written an internationally respected work on Old Turkic languages absolutely has to receive a National Prize.'

The Central Committee members are terribly sorry and look around for another prize for Hasso Grabner. Hasso Grabner himself, meanwhile, finds a rope.

The rope is made of wire and hangs, absolutely unrecognized in its symbolic dimension, from a crane due to be sent to the Soviet Union as a reparation payment. Now, though, in June 1951, the crane is not in Moscow but in Magdeburg and won't be going anywhere soon, that much is for sure, because a number of parts needed to finish making it are unavailable.

Two hundred kilometres south of Magdeburg, in Zwickau, meanwhile, is a finished coal shaft, but one of the machines inside it is not operational, missing – of course – a wire rope.

The coal miners from Zwickau – aware, for some inexplicable reason, of the rope hanging around doing nothing in Magdeburg – enquire with regard to the possibility of borrowing it at the Reparations Office, where – how could it be any other way? – Hasso Grabner is now based, having moved there after the dissolution of his crude iron, steel and rolling-mills federation, now working as a senior department head.

Grabner, sworn in by the Great Church of Communism yet inspired, as it were, by the Holy Ghost of pragmatic unconventionality, finds the Zwickau coal miners' request absolutely legitimate and sees no problem in it. The crane is not yet finished, after all, and aside from that, if a country wants to pay reparations, it must also be in a position to mine the necessary products to do so. So he delivers the rope – and soon finds himself tied up in knots. The party suspects Hasso Grabner of profiteering.

It is one of the usual ironies of Grabner's story. The man recommended to the Reparations Office on the grounds that his past career consisted partly of implementing the orders of the Soviet military administration and 'picking up and punishing profiteers and black marketeers' who were disrupting the construction of publicly-owned industry is now accused of profiteering himself, declared a disturber of the German-Soviet reparations-based peace by the SED, and dismissed. The rope is only a pretext in the matter, merely the material used to string Grabner up; it had already been deducted from the German reparations account, the official statement states, and thereby had been irreversibly made over to the Soviets – and as everyone knows, a gift is a gift, you can't take it back.

So there he dangles, Hasso Grabner, upside-down from a rope. He looks like a human wrecking ball. Yet he's the one being wrecked. Bit by bit, the party's cadre department strips him of his history, and that starts at the skeletal level: ideology.

As it says in one of the numerous political character reports the party has been pre-emptively commissioning for years (that is, for a possible *bending* or – we're talking bones, after all – breaking of Party Member number 185328), reports now fetched out of the depths of his cadre file, Grabner has long since left the foundations of Marxism-Leninism. Instead, he is allegedly ruled by a purely pragmatic sense of reason, oriented solely along practical lines and theoretically underpinned, if at all, merely by Trotskyist tizzies and Bukharinist ballyhoo, for which reason it is no surprise that Grabner denies the absolutely irrefutable theory of the impoverishment of the working class in capitalism – he is documented as saying that the workers in West Germany have 'a high standard of living'. And not only that. He made a joke out of the leading role of the working class in a lecture ('The worker is against the stopwatch, not against the clock; how else is he to know when it's time to knock off?') and also stated he had only read the works of Marx and Engels on holiday and even then 'not quite smoothly' – and, last but not least, also mocked scientific socialism and the GDR's national economic plans, declaring in retrospect, with regard to the 1948 half-year plan: 'We had no experience, no documents, they just jotted down a few lines on a sheet of paper and that was the 1948 half-year plan.'

All that spells trouble. Even though that's the way history goes. A succession of banalities that escalates into a drama every time... Churchill, who spontaneously sketches his ideas about the future division of the Balkans on half a sheet of paper and gets Stalin to sign off on it no less spontaneously. The economic functionaries in the Soviet-occupied zone write themselves a wish-list without a hint of a plan and get the people to work it off in the hope that their wishes may take on the appearance of a plan, at least in the eyes of the people.

And in actual fact, the people really do regard the numbers jotted down on paper as a plan. If someone comes along and tells them it's not a plan at all, only a pseudo-empirical number salad with an ink dressing, they refuse to believe him, even if that same someone admits he prepared the salad himself. But that's not the end of it. Certainly not for that part of the people who attend the party school. And least of all when the teacher's name is Hasso Grabner. When he gives a talk in November 1950 at the SED's cadre factory on 'The Tasks of the Party in the Fulfilment and Surpassing of the National Economic Plan' and takes the opportunity to relate the adventurous origins of the 1948 half-year plan, he first garners incredulous looks – and then experiences first-hand what it means to set his own practical experiences against the millions of wish-lists printed off by the SED.

Their faith in the plan and the party allegedly shaken, the students refuse to hear any more of Grabner's version of history ('He denied the real basis of our national economic plans!'), decline to follow his instructions ('A number of students spontaneously stopped taking notes.') and present him, having forced him to end his lecture, with their 'own' version of the making of plans ('Walter Ulbricht's article in the *Tägliche Rundschau* remains the benchmark for us.').

The consequence: the students, their faith not weakened to any great extent, declare that their faith is not faith but rather, exactly like the plan, nothing but the truth, built on strong foundations, tried by the party and tested by history, and on this basis they arrive at the conclusion that Hasso Grabner is a disseminator of false teachings who must be denounced to the Great Church of Communism.

In order for that to happen, the party students pick up their downed pens, write an indictment, title it 'Report', make the molehills of plan-making into a mountain and send it to the Central Party Control Commission, which, as the students know full well, collects and collates everything – prepared, pre-emptive, without pause.

No wonder the committee members have an embarrassment of riches to choose from when they delve deeper and deeper into Hasso Grabner's file in 1951, *the year of the rope*. And what they find only makes him sink lower in their eyes; Grabner has, as it turns out, violated the cadre-political principles of personnel policy on numerous past occasions and repeatedly employed 'human dregs' in the companies he ran.

For instance, not only has Grabner ('We are informed of his time in the fascist Wehrmacht.') employed CDU members, butter thieves and similarly dubious subjects, but he has also given jobs to former Nazi Party members and Wehrmacht soldiers and, in addition, handed out difficult-to-obtain permission slips for work trips to West Germany like bread coupons, which led to a number of his people only making the outbound journey.

In other words: 'In the choice of his employees, Comrade Grabner is not led by the principles of Leninism-Marxism, but his personal principles. Furthermore, he maintains links to a series of politically very dubious persons.' And just so that no one thinks Grabner's issue might be of a purely personnel-policy nature: 'We consider these false appointments, in conjunction with his previous behaviour, not only due to a lack of ideological clarity, but a marked tendency towards opposition politics.' With the addition, in Hasso Grabner's case, of 'moral deficits'. 'We can take our pick from his pearls of smut.'

There is certainly no sign of communist abstinence in Grabner's behaviour. Then again, he's not crouched in some knocked-up shack in the Greek mountains; he has an office in Berlin, drives from one factory to another and stays in various hotels, although he has a home, a wife, and by now two children in Leipzig. ('A character report from his local Borough Committee states that he has never shown an interest in his Residential Borough Committee.') Instead, there is constant womanising. And women turning up to work with bows in their hair. And men doing the same. And all that just because it's carnival season and 'Comrade Grabner goes along with every kind of nonsense.' Otherwise, though, he's rather strict with his staff and with himself even more so, often working 18 hours a day, making a bed of his staff car and a kitchen of his lunch box, setting up two dozen factories at a time and taking care, on top of that, that the Maxhütte steelworks – extremely important for the economy in the Soviet Occupation Zone* – gets a water supply, piped in uphill over six kilometres, in a third of the projected time.

Now and then, though, he lets it get on top of him, and then the ladies are allowed to go to the hairdresser during working hours, the men are allowed to go to the West, and the ordered course of things is allowed to go its own way, whereby the general impression is that Comrade Grabner considers proper channels nothing but non-binding guidelines written by pen-pushers.

In the party cadre department, in any case, they are less than ecstatic about such behaviour and conclude: 'It would be advisable to establish whether Comrade G. has already been assessed and what the Assessment Commission's findings are.'

The year is 1951, and the assessment is underway. Hasso Grabner is now 40 years old. He ought to be at the peak of his creativity. *Acme*, the Greek historiographers call it, while the Roman ones say *floret* – 'he is in full bloom'. But those writing Hasso Grabner's story in his present day of 1951 are neither Greeks nor Romans, but members of the Socialist Unity Party of Germany's Central Party Control Commission – and the only thing in full bloom for Hasso Grabner is a party penalty.

Before the verdict is reached, Hasso Grabner is allowed to state one last wish. Which he – modest as ever – proceeds to do:

'I would like to ask you to make the decision quickly. It doesn't matter to me what work I do. I don't want to run a company of 50 or 60 men just to secure my own existence. Then I'd prefer to be a labourer. I'm not out for any advantages, I'm out for being able to make a difference and work and develop my strengths, and then I'm a better or a happier man. I will probably write film manuscripts or a novel.'

The response from the Party Control Commission: 'That shows that this discussion has passed you by without a trace.'

Thus, the dice are cast and the time has come to tally up. The points from the past are added on top and form a line that clearly deviates from the correct path.

The verdict:
'Comrade Grabner shall receive a strict reprimand with removal of functions and shall enter the production process for two years. Central Party Control Commission, signed: Matern'

The fall of Hasso Grabner, one might think, is thus sealed. He is put into a foundry in the provinces to go on with life as a simple worker. Except that the people in the small workplace immediately notice that Grabner the trained bookseller might not be a good iron founder but he's all the better an organiser. So he gets promoted to factory manager. And gets the place producing 246% of its previous output in the space of 10 months.

The local party functionaries are delighted by the massive overcompliance to the plan and report the impressive feat directly to Berlin, where they believe first in a miracle, then in a discovery, and finally in nothing more at all. When the SED heads find out who is responsible for the increased performance, the smiles soon turn upside down – and Hasso Grabner gets his next party slap on the wrist. Because he didn't go into production as instructed, he is demoted to an *unskilled* foundry worker and shortly after that – because there's always space to sink lower – to an unskilled fitter, and stuck in a light metalworks firm whose manager is guaranteed not to let anyone take his job.

Which he doesn't do. But there are others who won't let anyone take things from them. Steel barons, for example. By 1953, a number of steelworks companies in the GDR have still not been nationalised. In order to change that, to turn the factories into public property, the SED needs someone who knows his way around expropriation. But who could that be?

The party leaders in Berlin think it over, seeking the right man here, there, and all over the republic. And don't find one. After a while they're at a loss. And that's the moment when they ask Hasso Grabner if he wouldn't mind...

He wouldn't mind, and he goes right ahead. Thus, the freshly dismissed unskilled fitter is commissioned by the party in April 1953 to buy up 'or otherwise obtain' half a dozen steelworks.

Hasso Grabner gets to work right away.
The party puts all his penalties on pause.
The Soviets object.

Not to Hasso Grabner, his penalties or their absolution, but to the party. The SED, so it's said in the Kremlin in May '53, has overdone it with the whole socialisting thing. A new course is required, and make it snappy. So the SED heads are summoned to Moscow in early June, presented with pelmeni, instructions and a paper containing 'measures for the convalescence of the political situation in the GDR', return home – without pelmeni but with plenty of bellyache – don't know quite what to do with themselves once they get there, and on 9 June, under strict retention of the production-target increases declared at the end of May, pass a, ahem, 'New Course'.

And Hasso Grabner? Once again, he's in the wrong place at the wrong time. Or perhaps the place is right and only the time is wrong. Or the time's just fine and the place is no good. Whatever the case, it simply doesn't work out. The former pig-iron king who became a labourer is no longer allowed to expropriate the steel barons, according to directives from Moscow, and the only thing Hasso Grabner can do after history has once again veered off course is to write a new résumé and declare a little wistfully: 'I nationalised only two companies.'

The party, meanwhile, declares in its newspaper: 'We have made mistakes.'

Seeing as the production-target increases don't fall into the mistake category for now, a few dozen builders down tools in Berlin on 16 June 1953, grab the bricks intended for the construction of the Stalinallee boulevard, decide they can be used for other purposes, march across town with them and throw them at various party and government buildings.

The next day, hundreds of thousands follow their example all over the republic. Not all armed with bricks but many of them possessing old bed sheets, they take the latter, write slogans on them and march around the towns with them, protesting at the top of their voices against the SED leaders and presenting the government cowering in a Berlin bunker with their own measures for the convalescence of the political situation in the GDR.

When the Bolshevik birdbrains in the bunker hear about that, they get not only bellyaches but headaches as well, and they remember their visit to Moscow and how the Soviets still have a few tanks and soldiers stationed in the country. High time to see whether they're still in good working order after all these years…

The rest is history. A popular uprising, pacified Moscow-style. After that, continual commemorations, historiographical reinterpretations, all neatly divided depending on the state of the nation. Official remembering. Unofficial forgetting. Anyone who can, stays out of it. Anyone who can't, dies off.

Hasso Grabner, meanwhile, returns from Berlin to Leipzig, finds out that the local Socialist Unity Party functionary Paul Fröhlich gave orders to shoot three hours *before* the state of emergency was declared, sees them carrying a 19-year-old through the streets in his coffin, starts to feel his constant rewriting of résumés is pointless, seeing as history is repeating itself anyway, and gets appointed by the party as director of a mining company with 800 employees, as always because no one else is available. In other words: the erstwhile pig-iron king is now a brown-coal prince.

At least in the eyes of his employees, who not only see Grabner sitting in his office well into the evening hours, but also spot him early in the morning, standing at the works gates and checking their punctuality. Alongside all that, Grabner also conducts the works choir, and when numerous villages around Leipzig threaten to sink into the mud-brown floods of the White Elster river in 1954, he picks up pick and shovel and helps his staff dig drainage ditches and build makeshift bridges. As a result, Grabner's employees soon think of him as a master of all trades, who seems to be in several places at once and apparently never tires.

Hasso Grabner sees things a little differently, however, and says so not only to the party, but also in one of his later résumés: 'I did not feel fully engaged and I made that clear. In the spring of 1954, the Politburo decided to install a general contractor and investment officer for all brown coal mines in the GDR, and granted me this position in addition to my role as mine director.'

Before that, however, something else unexpected happens; on 12 November 1953, Hasso Grabner's father puts in a sudden appearance. He alights from section eight of a personnel sheet marked 'Confidential!' – the form the brown-coal prince Hasso Grabner has to fill out for his application for the office of coal king. The father doesn't have a date of birth, but we do at least now know his name. It is Moritz Obermann, and under 'most recent activity', Hasso Grabner notes down: 'deceased'.

He has thus left the sphere of the living behind him ('car accident'), while history repeats itself once again for his son. Like six years before in the realms of steel and iron, Hasso Grabner now rules over tens of thousands in brown-coal land, people who break open the earth and bulldoze out the billions. Or, as Grabner writes with something approaching awe: 'From one day to the next, I was managing 52 major construction sites.'

The best of prerequisites to fail miserably – or to win prizes. And lo and behold: 'I was nominated for the 'Hero of Labour' award for 1954 and '55.'

But because Hasso Grabner doesn't exactly suffer from low self-esteem ('When giants are called, it's not dwarfs who respond.') and the SED top brass officially cannot stand kings, or at least do not accept any who rule the country alongside them, the idea of the prize for the brown-coal king soon goes up in smoke.

'My relationship to Comrade Paul Fröhlich, tense from the outset, was to blame. I was arrogant enough to believe I could afford it, and Comrade Fröhlich lacked the magnanimity to laugh it off.'

And now? Uprising? Suppression? Regicide? After all, it's not long ago that Comrade Paul Fröhlich was giving orders to shoot. He's also a member of the appeals council in the SED's Central Committee, and only the party knows how quickly granting grace can turn into a coup de grâce. In short: there are a number of indications that, compared with the house of correction in Waldheim, the names at the Leipzig party headquarters have rather different priorities…

A hundred and fifty kilometres east of Leipzig, in a place named Schwarze Pumpe* – Black Pump – it's not bullets being fired but bricks being laid. And plenty of them. Here, on the margins of the Lusatian coal district, is 'the biggest building site in the republic,' 'the most important undertaking in realising the key goal of the five-year plan,' 'the major industrial complex that will solve the GDR's energy problem,' 'the key operation for the whole country.' Only unfortunately, it's not exactly turnkey ready, if not to say it doesn't yet actually exist at all.

But that changes, as on 31 August 1955 Fritz Selbmann, familiar with exploratory drilling as a former miner, and a highly representative figure due to his status as minister of heavy industry, turns the first shovel – with a bulldozer.

The usual ceremony follows. A woman in traditional dress offers the customary bread and salt, the minister helps himself, the crowd cheers, journalists document the situation, the guests of honour raid the buffet, the workers clean up after them.

Once it's all over, along comes a writer and asks questions.

'Who will build this fabled Schwarze Pumpe? Who will conjure bustling open-cast mines out of these long-ranging pine woods, who will make tall chimneys, loud turbines and generators grow out of this heath, who will get 60,000 tons of petrol, more precious than the freshest water, flowing out of the pipes of Schwarze Pumpe every year?'

Seeing as no one wants to talk to the writer, as usual, and purely imaginary answers are banned in the piece of writing he has to deliver, this despite the fact that the five-year plan proclaims similarly positive prospects, he turns for help to the party, which always has a few fresh young staff available to take care of such special cases, young men who are dispensable, in case they end up burned out – it is a coal-fired power station, after all.

Now that he has the party faithful bowing and scraping around him, no one wants to talk to the writer all the more, and the heat is soon on. But seeing as the power station's not yet ready for operation, no one gets their fingers burnt at least, and with the aid of a trade-union functionary, the writer, having introduced himself only as 'Herr Bronnen', does manage in the end to make a contact, and he soon enters 'the most sacred room of the highest man, the construction director of Schwarze Pumpe.' Who, of course – how could it be any other way? – is Hasso Grabner.

Grabner can't tell, however, that the man suddenly standing in the doorway is a harmless writer. In any case, all his odd enquiries soon make a negative impression, so much so that Grabner begins to wonder who sent the guy to his office. Confronted with this question, the writer reels off a list of names, titles and organisations, but none of them interest Grabner in the slightest. He picks up the telephone and instructs the factory security team to have the oddball in his office arrested.

It's down to Karl Heinrich Stein that it doesn't come to that, the little Jewish fellow from Buchenwald who was really called Steinitz, a writer who found his own work in Hasso Grabner's camp library. Steinitz may have been dead for more than 10 years, but Grabner still remembers him, and when he hears that the man in his office is a writer and comes from Vienna, just like Steinitz, he turns over a new leaf and starts telling concentration-camp stories.

Mr Bronnen the writer not having come to hear that kind of thing, Hasso Grabner eventually does tell him a bit about the construction work. Now, though, 60 years later, Grabner's words about Buchenwald are mixed up with those Arnolt Bronnen noted down about Schwarze Pumpe: 'Grabner points out of the window of his barrack into the dusk-black woods: "The briquetting plant will be there, the hydration complex there, the power station there, the administration wing will be built here…" I see only woods; he sees more.'

Once Bronnen has gone, I'm alone with Grabner. He's standing with his back to me, rummaging through a heap of paper – and I catch myself only now wondering how Grabner actually got here. Probably, I suspect, Selbmann had something to do with it. It was probably his old jail-mate who got him the job here. And what do you know, after a while I find an old photo. It's dated 31 August 1955, the day of the ground-breaking ceremony, the day when Selbmann used the bulldozer.

The photo shows Grabner with a file and papers under his arm. He's standing directly next to Selbmann, who is just being handed the traditional bread by a woman in Sorbian costume and is trying to break it. Yet Selbmann looks anything but good. He comes across as clumsy, overly cautious, almost anxious, as if scared to press too hard, as though the woman were putting not bread but a baby into his hands and he, the heavy, the minister of heavy industry, were scared of breaking it. He reaches out as carefully as he can, hunching his shoulders – and that makes him look altogether ministerially heavy, yet more wooden, bulkier, more colossal than usual. Even the bulldozer next to him seems too small for him, and I wonder why they didn't just give him a piece of land so that he could break it open with his huge hands and fetch the coal out while he's at it. He could always have eaten the bread afterwards.

And Grabner? He's standing there, watching his ungainly minister friend. And laughing. And not yet realising he'll be on his own once Selbmann is gone.

But he already is on his own; although the enormous construction project begins in the summer of 1955, thus granting the future legend its foundation, there is no end of shortages in Schwarze Pumpe. They're short on managerial staff for the undertaking and on accommodation for the workers, some project plans not drawn up until *after* they're constructed or not arriving on site at all, which is not all that bad in fact because they're short on material anyway. And on machines. Or both. In any case, Schwarze Pumpe is soon dominated by the untainted rule of wishful thinking, each individual only able to stand up against the still uncompleted object through the power of imagination, threatened morning after morning by powerlessness in the face of dreams, the individual completely disconnected, the legend ended – the banalities of another day.

At least that's what it's like for those incapable of taking action. Grabner, however, is capable. Aware that there are 600 carpets lying fallow in one of his old factories somewhere, an unsellable pilot run that in his opinion would pass as first-class goods in West Germany, and knowing a few others in the same region would cough up a whole lot of shingle for a few tons of filtered gravel, he takes the direct route as usual, gets the rugs and the rocks exported (with the relevant permission) and two weeks later has enough money in the bank to buy the machines so desperately needed to build Schwarze Pumpe. However, the state-owned domestic and foreign commerce company in charge of placing orders forgets to send said machinery orders to the Soviet Union, and Grabner is condemned to inactivity, despite all the riches. For a few days, at least. After that, he simply orders the devices he needs in West Germany, which leads to exactly the heavy construction machinery being delivered to his door that the GDR has been banned from importing by the Americans.

When it comes to the desperately needed managerial staff, however, there's not much Hasso Grabner can do – the jobs at that level are only given to SED members, for which reason he's soon complaining to the relevant party committees and informing them that not only are there not enough workers, materials and project plans on the building site, but also there's no technical manager, no senior bookkeeper and not even a director of labour. The party promises to send managerial staff, but not a single one arrives at Schwarze Pumpe during Grabner's whole time in office. And the government also seems strangely uninterested in building the industrial complex, now that the act has been passed to do so. The Central Committee mediator, at least, acknowledges all Grabner's suggestions and descriptions with nothing but shrugs, while the responsible undersecretary of state doesn't show his face a single time on site, preferring to spend his time sitting in his Berlin office and rejecting Grabner's staff proposals out of hand, every one of them.

The construction site, meanwhile, keeps growing and growing, with 12,000 people soon toiling away there, while the works canteen can only churn out 1000 portions a day and the un-catered-for can't even go to bed with empty bellies at night because there aren't enough beds to go around. What is to be done? Get them working in three shifts and re-introduce rotating bed occupation? One room, four beds, twelve men and eight hours for each of them?

Hasso Grabner doesn't even consider such a thing. Building in the 20th century for the 21st century means you can't rest on any 19th-century laurels. He has to do something. Here and now. And so, in January 1956, Hasso Grabner writes a Manifesto for the Accelerated Construction of Workers' Accommodation, sends it to the relevant committee and hopes the party will react better to paper plans than to real-life needs.

It doesn't. The party is still the party, and in times of need it reacts only to thrown stones, not to paper. Aside from that it's winter, and all activities in Schwarze Pumpe have come to a standstill. Not only in programmatic terms, but also in actuality.

The temperatures plunge in early February '56, as suddenly as skaters who venture onto the ice too soon plunge and plummet to the bottom of the thermometer where they stay for weeks on end, frozen stiff, while the East wind blows up top, cutting and cold. Russian winter. Siberian shock. Nothing works all over the land. Even Schwarze Pumpe lies still. It is the coldest month in human memory.

When the worst is over at the beginning of March, it is Hasso Grabner's turn to take a tumble. An extremely painful trigeminal neuralgia forces him to see a doctor. The doctor forces Hasso Grabner to stay in bed. Hasso Grabner forces himself to the nearest telephone and attempts 'to manage the construction remotely'.

In Schwarze Pumpe, meanwhile, nothing is working any more. But because the complex is too important for the GDR, and the number of bricks stored on the construction site is too large, the SED Politburo decides to hold a meeting on the subject on 4 April. Grabner is invited, but he considers the draft resolution unhelpful and proposes a large number of changes, which results in a proposal for change to suddenly involve him. The Cottbus Party Committee, geographically responsible for Schwarze Pumpe, demands Grabner's dismissal during the meeting. Walter Ulbricht himself intervenes and will hear nothing of toppling the construction director. That puts an end to the meeting, and since the draft resolution hasn't been passed, the problems at Schwarze Pumpe haven't been cleared up and the chaos has essentially only got worse, the solution is – what else? – to form a commission.

This commission is charged with writing a new draft, but the group's composition soon changes in a very strange manner. And when Grabner's advocate Selbmann unexpectedly leaves the commission without explanation, suddenly eliminated, Grabner once again becomes the object of an investigation with a clear aim formulated with maximum clarity: Grabner, the group declares unanimously, is to surrender his position. Without delay.

By the time the Politburo next discusses Schwarze Pumpe a week later, Hasso Grabner's career is over. Instead of talking about the problems on the construction site, several members of the commission have used their time there to obtain information on Grabner, to tie them in with items from his party file and to present these complete works to Ulbricht to point out that Grabner is 'ideologically untenable'. Not being fond of discussions by nature, but unable to simply overlook the matter in view of the remnants of political culture still in place in the Politburo for formal reasons, Ulbricht determines that the decision on Grabner's future is 'to be clarified down there,' which is where it falls – and Grabner along with it.

The justification for Grabner's sacking is basically the same one he got five years previously: cadre policy according to personal rather than Marxist-Leninist principles, veering off the party line in behavioural matters, ideological unclarities, moral weaknesses. There's a new one, though: a couple of hundred Italian guest workers. And yet Grabner's need for them was for absolutely socialist reasons. He reads in the newspaper at the end of 1955 that West German capitalists are recruiting labour in Italy, an idea which in Grabner's view is not great in ideological terms but pretty practical in practical terms, all the more so because he can't go to Italy himself but is in urgent need of labour. Why not, he asks himself, start his own little recruitment campaign and steer the newly arrived Italians straight from West Germany on to 'Pompa Negra'? After all, they'd only be serving the imperialist monopoly capitalists in West Germany, but in the GDR they could be helping to build socialism and gaining practical experience in a country where the workers are in charge.

The upshot of Grabner's plan: the cadre craniums in the party now consider him not only a sectarian, but also an 'adventurer and fantasist', chucking him out with the explanation:

> Comrade Hasso Grabner has been dismissed from his role as construction director on the suggestion of the Combine Party Committee, because he did not offer a guarantee for the success of the construction of the "Schwarze Pumpe" industrial complex.
> Pumpe, 7 April 1956,
> Signed: Bumbel

Bumbel from Pumpe has spoken, and while I'm still trying to make sense out of that name, I suddenly realise why Bronnen wrote right at the beginning of his report on Schwarze Pumpe that Grabner had taken on the task 'on an interim basis'. By the time Bronnen publishes his *Journey of Discovery around the German Democratic Republic* at the end of 1956, Grabner has already been sacked, but Bronnen's piece about him is finished. Bronnen can't just cut Grabner out – that would entail eliminating Schwarze Pumpe and robbing the legend under construction of its story, which, as the party's legend-layers know all too well, is the condition for the possibility of its projected permanent existence. So Bronnen has to retrospectively add what he didn't see coming during his visit, a destiny that was never in place. The solution means calling him something absolutely atypical for a legend, 'on an interim basis'.

Thus, it comes to pass that Hasso Grabner is not only dismissed, but is also unemployed on the First of May, the day of the working man's struggle. Officially, however, there is no unemployment in the GDR (and Walter Ulbricht has an unsuspected guilty conscience over the construction director's downward delegation), so the Secretary General of the SED Politburo makes his second intervention into Grabner's case in a matter of weeks and instructs his ministers to 'deploy the man according to his abilities'.

As all parties are aware, these abilities lie not in theoretical prognostication, but in practical organisation, and Grabner is hence appointed by the GDR minister of chemistry in October 1956 as deputy director of a large state-owned construction and engineering bureau. There, however, he is under special surveillance due to the story now on his files. The usual routine follows.

'Although Comrade Grabner is a very intelligent man with a gift for speaking, the party organisation has unfortunately established that he suffers from a major lack of ideological clarity.'

To make quite sure everyone gets the message:

'He attempted to convince the comrades on the party committee of the allegedly high standard of living for the working class in West Germany, and came to the conclusion that there can be no further thought of a class struggle or a revolutionary movement in West Germany, and that the law discovered by Marx of the absolute immiseration of the working class under capitalism no longer applies.'

Hasso Grabner is thus no longer under special surveillance; Hasso Grabner is out on his ear. And the undersecretary of state who's had his beady eyes on him for a while and now also sends him the letter of dismissal is, of course, an eagle named Adler.

The appropriate party penalty is not far behind. And here too, it's the usual routine: official reprimand, removal from his role, and off to the production line for two years.

Various party functionaries lodge protests, however, and Hasso Grabner's career as an unskilled labourer is not continued. One of the protesters, having been in Waldheim with Grabner, is now head of the Central Committee's agitation department and is desperately seeking someone to put in charge of an exhibition marking the 40th anniversary of the October Revolution, so he appoints Hasso Grabner – who hasn't asked for the favour and can't do anything about it – as editor-in-chief. Seeing as the exhibition is staged in Leipzig and Grabner's archenemy Paul Fröhlich is still king of the heap there, he's up to his neck in trouble in the blink of an eye – and six months later, the usual remarks are entered in his file for the fourth time over: official reprimand, removal from his role, and off to the production line for two years.

And yet this time it's different, because Hasso Grabner protests. He sees no reason why he should be degraded to an unskilled labourer all over again, especially not when the Central Party Control Commission's verdict is signed by the same man who sent him to the provinces on behalf of the party as a foundry worker in 1951, and in 1953 – on behalf of the same party – made him a steel baron. Hasso Grabner can't be bothered any more with all this nonsense – and he unceremoniously declares himself a freelance writer.

I did not want to become a writer but I had no other option.

Hasso Grabner, note on file on the occasion of a discussion with
the Leipzig Party Control Commission,
4 April 1966

Spelling It Out

And so he picks up his pen, but actually Hasso Grabner has always been writing. Agitprop texts, poems, songs, political screeds, newspaper articles on the latest production methods... in *Neues Deutschland*, the SED's party newspaper, alone there are dozens of pieces written by Grabner. Most of them are entitled things like 'The Struggle for the Improvement of Steel Quality', with the sub-header: 'No objective difficulties'.

Of course, there are subjective difficulties, as Hasso Grabner has learned well enough by now. In the struggle for the improvement of ideological steadfastness, the party has several times declared him an uncertain prospect. But Hasso Grabner wouldn't be Hasso Grabner if he were to stop polarising now that he's a writer, were he even able to stop at all.

When he is admitted to the Writers' Association in autumn 1958 – after the publication of his short story 'The Row over the Partisans' – he is certified as having 'strong literary talent'. But that's only one side of the coin, the other being: 'All in all, Comrade Hasso Grabner gives the contradictory impression of a talented egotist.'

A talented egotist – that has to be a contradiction for the socialist writers' functionaries, at least in political terms, because in artistic terms they do value bourgeois aestheticism's ideas of art and purity. However, Hasso Grabner has a bad rap sheet on exactly this point, and is constantly being awkward, or in other words: 'His relationship to his own literary work is characteristic for him.

Among comrades, he assesses his work almost exclusively according to the material benefits it brings him.'

There it is again, that old familiar Grabnerist pragmatism, purer than any art can ever be. And yet this time there's a problem, because the second literary work that Grabner presents in 1958 is certainly no bestseller. His poetry collection *The Stroke Is on the Left Foot*, published just in time for the Christmas rush (and for the KPD's 40th anniversary) sells only nine copies in all of Leipzig's bookshops by the end of December.

Is it down to the poems? There are no obvious objective difficulties, at least, and Grabner's subjective standpoint is also of unimagined clarity. There's not a trace of ideological contradiction, even between the lines. Quite the contrary. Grabner's poems are single-stroke engines in paper form, not exactly quiet operators and occasionally running less than smoothly, if not to say *jolting all over the page*, but equipped with a clearly left-handed flywheel, which, once it gets started, unremittingly sets the direction. 'Onward!'

Essentially, reading the last three poems in the little book is enough. They all end with the words: 'Socialism shall be victorious.'

Then again, what use is even the most wonderful socialism if it doesn't sell? Nine copies sold is not enough to build an empire upon for the freelance writer Hasso Grabner, not even in the GDR.

That's how 1958 ends – and by the time I run into Hasso Grabner again at the beginning of January, he's no longer sitting at a desk, but standing in a factory.

Have they put him on a production line after all? Or did he go of his own accord, perhaps? Because he realised that his left-footed lyric poetry helped him to propagate his country's future but not to secure his own?

One might think so, but that's not the case. Hasso Grabner, the writer, wouldn't be Hasso Grabner, the chronicler of the grotesque named history, if he weren't always exactly in the place where that grotesque is made, if not to say *fabricated*. In this case, that's the aluminium works of the Bitterfeld Electrochemical Combine. Right there, where life is a chemically reduced gigantic state-owned corpus, where the world consists of nothing but cold concrete constructions, cloud-producing industrial chimneys and endlessly winding pipes, and where the GDR is so grey that even black-and-white photos can't capture the dreariness, all members of the Nikolai Mamai Youth Brigade are standing beside a steaming electrolysis tank in a hall the size of a football field – and looking for the Book of the Month.

Is that why Hasso Grabner is here? Does he want to flog his poetry collection to the young workers? Having once worked in the iron and steel industry himself and now, as a poet, written the classic 'Ballad of the Construction of the Gröditz Ring Rolling Mill'? The youth brigade's goal is, after all, 'for every member to collect a home library of literature'. So why shouldn't they...

But of course, none of that is true at all. That is, the Youth Brigade does indeed gather around the electrolysis tank on that 3 January 1959. And Hasso Grabner is there too. And they really are talking about literature, but all these are mere building blocks in the actual story. The 'Mamais', Hasso Grabner and literature are merely means to the end of a far larger performance. That began a month previously, on 3 December 1958, in the Berlin bureau of the Chairman of the Free German Trade Union Federation, Herbert Warnke.

On that day, Warnke, subject to major internal criticism from the SED leaders and considered (along with his unified trade union) politically disoriented, lacking in initiative and largely incapable in general, has a visit from a delegation of Soviet trade unionists, who tell him about a new movement calling itself 'Communist Labour Brigades'. According to the Russians, almost bursting with pride, the members have set themselves the goal of working and living in such a way that 'the great personal responsibility for the common cause of building communism is visible in all their actions.'

Warnke soon realises that the movement, allegedly emerged from the ranks of the workers and spreading across the Soviet territories in a flush of spontaneous enthusiasm, was in actual fact initiated by the leadership of the Communist Party of the Soviet Union, but that doesn't bother him. On the contrary. He imagines the exact same thing for the GDR, except that it cannot be the CPSU that starts the ball rolling, but the trade union federation. And his stock has to start rolling, Warnke knows all too well; after all, the movement originated in a Moscow shunting station – and he, Herbert Warnke, has no wish to be shunted aside in East Berlin's political railyard.

There follows a precisely planned script based on an article on the brigades movement in the Soviet Union, published in *Pravda* on 10 December and immediately translated into German, which Warnke partly transcribes verbatim, merely replacing the word 'communist' with 'socialist'. The demands and objectives mentioned in the *Pravda* article are also largely borrowed by Warnke: promotion of the youth brigades, progressive increases of the labour targets, expansion of socialism beyond the world of work to the whole of life, and – of course – no fuss and nonsense!

To make sure the latter really doesn't happen (and to get Warnke firmly back on the right track), he quickly sprinkles a couple of Walter Ulbricht's 'Ten Commandments of Socialist Morals and Ethics' into the text and sends the script to the trade union federation's board of directors on 15 December, at which point it immediately starts circulating and ends up – by some miracle – reaching the central council of the Free German Youth and the Socialist Unity Party's leadership, whereupon everyone congratulates each other on this 'bottom-up' initiative, raising their hands in mulled-wine-soaked seasonal cheer and voting unanimously: 'The movement shall begin with an appeal from a youth brigade at the Bitterfeld Combine, to be published on 6 January at the latest.'

Before that, however, there is still plenty to be done. After all, as the engineers of the socialist worker's soul know all too well, even the best planned of spontaneous movements runs the risk of provoking unplanned reactions, for which reason not only is the entire Bitterfeld Youth Brigade instructed (and kept from working) through countless meetings, consultations and discussions from 30 December on (plus the usual New Year's Eve drinking session), but a general information ban is also put in place; after all, it's supposed to look like the spontaneous movement emerged directly on the shop floor, in this case around a steaming electrolysis tank.

> Electrolysis refers to the corrosion or conversion of a material by means of electrical current. It is a process of enforced reaction.

The only person who doesn't get wind of all this is the man at the very top, the man by the name of Walter Ulbricht, who merrily plans to announce the formation of socialist labour brigades in his New Year article – and only by making use of his new right track straight to the Politburo does Warnke manage to have the offending sentence struck shortly before publication, although he refrains from reminding Ulbricht of the eleventh commandment ('Thou shalt wait!').

That doesn't mean the preparatory measures, aimed at eliminating chance and simultaneously increasing authenticity, are complete;

before the Bitterfeld Brigade is allowed to read out 'their' appeal 'Working, Learning, Living as Socialists!' over the combine's public address system on 5 January, the trade union heads carry out various consultations with the press, radio and television, their purpose absolutely clear but apparently requiring spelling out nonetheless: 'It must be ensured that the press reacts immediately and correctly.'

Immediately and, from his perspective, certainly correctly is how Hasso Grabner reacts too. Having received 'friendly information' – from the *Tribüne* newspaper, he says – of important meetings held at the Bitterfeld Combine in early January, he hurries to the factory complex in question, arriving on the morning of 3 January 1959, and promptly adopts the role of chronicler.

Grabner plans to make a radio and television play out of the brigade's socialist wishes. Whether he is aware of being part of a rigged game, essentially a mad performance, only Grabner can say, if at all. But there are a number of indications that he has not been told about the secret script, which is why he believes, in fact has no other option but to believe, that 'the grand idea of the socialist brigade was discussed for the first time' on 3 January, the date of his arrival.

What is clear is that Grabner accompanies the Mamais along their path from that point on – from the reading of their voluntary commitment over the PA ('We have set ourselves the goal of working, learning and living in a socialist manner, to become a brigade of "socialist labour"') via the printing of the appeal in the press ('The trade union federation's daily newspaper reports') all the way to the subsequent reactions as scheduled in the script ('In the days following the issue of the appeal, the declarations of the next five brigades shall be published up to 10 January, along with the approving declarations of their departments' foremen and technical engineers.').

And while the people across the land are rejoicing over the workers' initiative, so joyful that they can't stop setting up socialist brigades, Hasso Grabner stays in Bitterfeld, in the football-field-sized hall of Aluminium Works I, and runs from one steaming electrolysis tank to the next with a pad of paper in one hand and a technical dictionary in the other. In their appeal, the Mamais called upon the members of the Unity Collective to engage in socialist competition – and it is Hasso Grabner's task to document that battle from both sides.

What presents itself in this manner over a matter of weeks is part of a prefabricated future, of which Hasso Grabner obviously isn't aware, as the subtitle to his account reveals a very different understanding, heralding 'the future we are already living in'.

The play, which portrays the competition between the two brigades, is written, acted and broadcast before the winter is out. It is a play in which the pragmatist Hasso Grabner beats the literature lover Hasso Grabner hands down, by technical knockout in the first act. And while the man of letters Hasso Grabner is down on the mat, the pragmatist Hasso Grabner stands on stage and describes his work to the reverently wide-eyed audience: 'The play is not about profound conflicts. No one shouts in it; it is about how people from two brigades behave towards each other in various situations.'

The audience nods its collective head, and the writers in its ranks also have plenty to listen to; Hasso Grabner informs them that his work was already broadcast in March '59 and that the special radio version of such a play has many advantages: 'I can only recommend everyone work with our radio-drama colleagues. Not least because present-day problems can be addressed in a relatively short time. Just think how long it takes before something like this is printed, unless a newspaper publishes it.'

What the newspapers do publish, however, is the Mamais' statement. The first paper to print the youth brigade's appeal is the *Tribüne*, that same newspaper that was 'friendly' enough to inform Hasso Grabner previously. And it is the *Tribüne* again that releases his play in printed form a year later through its book publishing house, under the title *Who Would Give Away a Victory?* – after it won the Free German Trade Union Federation's literary award in 1959.

Coincidence? Luck? Talent? Contacts? The files have nothing to say on the matter – and I don't care. For me, it's enough to know that Hasso Grabner, the writer, the chronicler of the grotesque named history, always finds himself precisely where that grotesque is being made.

After all that has happened, there can be no doubt that he himself is part of that grotesque, and if there is still doubt, then it is eliminated on 23 April 1959, because on that date – 200 kilometres east of Bitterfeld – the entire smelting-furnace collective at the Stalin Works in Stalinstadt is sat down in front of a tape recorder, spending its brigade evening listening to Hasso Grabner's play.

That listening session is only the beginning, however. It is continued in a seven-part literary concoction written by the socialist workers themselves and printed in the Stalin Works' internal newssheet. It is a novel with the title: *The Welder's Path to the Communist Labour Brigade: On the Life of the Grigori Sitalo Youth Brigade, Dnepropetrovsk*. It is no longer available in any literary library.

And Hasso Grabner? Not only is he part of the grotesque named history and always precisely where it is being made; he is also co-writing it, even though he doesn't know the script, and history is more than slippery, what with it only ever coming about once it's already happened…

Never mind. The workers in Hasso Grabner's play certainly all act as though Ulbricht's Ten Commandments have become part of their own flesh and blood. They live by the strict rules of the Great Church of Socialism 24 hours a day, they're more preachy than preachers, more reasonable than reason, and they have more of an education addiction than a communist in a prison library, condemned to all the free time in the world. They are, in a word, Hasso Grabner's written but not lived self, and it's no wonder that, once the performance is over and the whole sideshow has moved on, the Nikolai Mamai Brigade doesn't end up receiving the promised National Prize, just like Hasso Grabner didn't get it eight years previously.

Until then, however – that is, until the Mamais can revive their old drinking culture, skip reading the newspaper every day and go back to happily cutting corners and skimping on the job – the super-socialism in the Bitterfeld Electrochemical Combine officially goes on. After all, the SED's Central Committee passed a resolution in November 1958: 'Chemistry gives us bread, prosperity and beauty.' Whereby the beauty part, or rather the depiction of beauty, is still down to the writers – for it's all fiction, isn't it? – for the foreseeable future.

Seeing as one of them, Hasso Grabner, is already in Bitterfeld, and the Electrochemical Combine possesses a large Palace of Culture equipped with all mod cons, and the SED leadership has nothing better to do (in other words: feels at home in large palaces and takes a lively interest in various types of cons), 700 writers and functionaries are swiftly invited over and carted into the House of Culture in large groups. The first Bitterfeld Congress is opened on 24 April 1959, with the stated goal of not only bringing writers and workers together, but also making workers into writers, which essentially means nothing other than workers storming the peaks of culture and writers descending to the troughs of everyday life.

Those peaks will have to be flattened and the troughs filled in later, when everything is different, when the old horrors are over and replaced by new horrors, so they can be part of history. But now, in April 1959, this has to go unsaid, *cannot* be said, in fact, as it would immediately have to be gainsaid. The Mitteldeutscher Verlag publishing house, which organised the conference in Bitterfeld, devoted itself at its preparatory meeting in November 1958 to the 'splendid programme of our chemical industry' and decided, in its analysis of this programme, to raise its own programme – literature – 'to a new, higher level'. That initially leads to partnerships between publishers and various chemical production facilities, then to a corresponding literary competition and finally to the wish to form workers' writing groups in the factories, following the motto 'Pick up your pen, fellow worker!' – or, this one also stolen from the Russians – 'Let us lay these word-bricks of ours!'

It's hard to say what Hasso Grabner thinks of the whole caboodle. He got first-hand experience at the Schwarze Pumpe industrial complex of what it's like when a writer goes to work on the shop floor. And if everybody starts doing it... Then again, only recently he was standing by an electrolysis tank and now he has already fulfilled what the Bitterfeld Conference calls for: operative literature on building socialism. In fact, he may well have pre-empted it, having written his *play on the future we are already living in*, even before the party declared that future to be the present in the first place. No wonder, then, that Hasso Grabner is not only allowed to speak at the Bitterfeld Conference and report on his experiences, but that his work is also praised – by Alfred Kurella, the head of the Culture Commission in the SED Central Committee's Politburo and, incidentally, the first and only proponent of a theory stating that humankind's first verses were composed while riding a camel.

But the SED is well aware that Grabner doesn't always live as he writes; that is, he may not be a cultural camel, but he is something of an ideological chameleon, so his radio play is quoted in Kurella's opening conference speech, but not noted. The minutes contain not a single word about Grabner's play. That part has been struck from the record.

And Grabner? He shrugs his shoulders, strolls out of the Palace of Culture and goes on undeterred. He writes the script for a film (*Dr Ahrendt's Decision*), composes an agitprop revue for the GDR Workers' Festival, leads a writing group for workers at the Leuna Chemical Works and a group of young authors in Leipzig, and publishes his next poetry collection directly after the Bitterfeld Conference, its title already giving the game away: *Fifteen Steps Straight Ahead*.

In parallel to his literary oeuvre, however, his Writers' Association file also begins to grow, and he is soon accused of 'megalomania'. Subjective difficulties, once again.

'Even in the Nazi era, he claims to have been a works manager in an 80-man factory for two years after his release from concentration camp until he was called up to the 999th, and to have practised constant sabotage. (These two years are skipped over in his résumé.)'

And lo and behold, those two years really are skipped over in the résumé he wrote for the Writers' Association, but Hasso Grabner did live through them. Just as he was the first person to have written a work of operative socialist literature in a state-owned production facility, even though that work is no longer mentioned by the party representatives in the documentation. Memory, that much is clear once and for all, is the basic fabric of history. Ideology, however, is the form in which history is written, struck out, abbreviated.

In Leuna, meanwhile, nothing is abbreviated; everything is written down – in the chemical works. In the workers' clubhouse. In the room where the Workers' Writing Circle meets. Things are written down one after another, duplicated from life directly onto paper, the writing workers, the men who crawl out from under huge pipes every Thursday evening and stick their heads of cadmium and quicksilver into the House of Culture, see the reflections of their chlorine-corroded faces on the freshly polished floors, walk its corridors as though they were paved with ice, until they open a door to find their peers sitting at school desks, writing.

This is the circle that Hasso Grabner runs. But it's not his first; he's done this before. Twenty years ago, in Buchenwald, in the concentration camp. Back then, they didn't describe the working days of a chemical worker; they talked about Lenin's *State and Revolution*. There were two of them in the circle back then, and it wasn't a matter of production problems in coal liquefaction; it was a matter of finding out something about the big picture and keeping the number of victims as small as possible. They didn't sit inside a House of Culture, between books and shelves, at desks above which heads gave off smoke and beneath which their removed work-boots steamed like the chimneys outside; they squatted down in the open air, on a felled tree, their shoes in the mud and everything at their feet a mush, and they talked instead of writing, always watchful that the wind didn't carry their words to the SS men.

In the Leuna clubhouse, however, all is absolutely silent, and as soon as the past week's manuscripts have been discussed, criticism made and suggestions given, the only sound is the scratch of pencil leads on grainy paper. The lights floating on the ocean of floor polish outside the door, meanwhile, don't move an inch, and the only thing that leaves the room of writing workers and gets through to the SED is two anthologies of their work.

And yet Hasso Grabner's experiment fails; most of the workers want neither to write about production-target fulfilment nor to be writers. Most of the workers simply want to know how to keep a brigade journal.

By 1965, the writing circle has shrunk down to two members. They were both there before Hasso Grabner. And they will be there after him too, they leave no room for doubt. In other words: Hasso Grabner is free to go.

Grabner leaves Leuna at the end of 1965. In the five years he spent there, he wrote six books. But now he's got the seven-year itch. He hasn't discovered any writers. But he has met a young woman. And published two collections, with the aid of the writing workers. Collections of poems, sketches of everyday life, photos, reports. They are texts in which heads are made of quicksilver, bodies are state-owned, and stories are boiled down to chemistry. Texts from a world in which the Houses of Culture are swimming in floor polish. Texts from the entirely fenced-in Leuna Works. The anthologies they are printed in both have the same name: *The New Song Starts Here*.

For Hasso Grabner, meanwhile, it's back to the same old tune; the party is unhappy – with the political and ideological state of the Writers' Association in general and with that of Hasso Grabner in particular. Whereby, in the view of the Marxist-Leninist cadre craniums, there's a direct connection between the two states; in this case – in contrast to the party committees' deductive directions – between micro and macro. In other words: Hasso Grabner gets another summons to the Regional Party Control Commission.

You might almost think Hasso Grabner did it on purpose. Seven against one, discussions for hours; he finally gets another chance to play the role of the heretic who argues with the party because he loves it so dearly.

'Infallibility,' he declares to the Regional Party Control Commission practically as soon as he crosses the threshold, 'is abhorrent to me.' And to make sure everyone gets the picture: 'I am not one of those people who consider art absolutely impossible if its creators don't live in accordance with its content. History knows more than one artist who drank like a fish and wrote like a god.'

He's thrown down the gauntlet. And while the Regional Party Control Commission members, not sure whether to take it up, start on the safe side by explaining that they're the Regional Party Control Commission members, I'm gradually getting the not-at-all negative feeling that Hasso Grabner the romantic is secretly and mischievously peeking out from behind the mask of Hasso Grabner the pragmatic. It's as if, while the workers in the House of Culture were writing about the practical uses of petrochemistry, he had been reading good old Schlegel, who even back then knew all about the antiorthodox, that is, *the true believers* – in the Great Church of Socialism and in any other church: 'The true Protestant,' writes Friedrich Schlegel in *Lessing from Leuna*, 'must also protest against Protestantism itself, whenever it wants to reverse itself into a new papacy and literalism. The freedom of thought knows no standstill, and polemics know no limits.'

By the devil, Hasso Grabner is always on board for a spot of polemics! Especially now that the Regional Party Control Commission has taken up the gauntlet and laid it on the table, albeit without informing Grabner – currently rattling his verbal sabre in anticipation ('In my blood I have a lust for arguing and enjoying pointed wit.') – that it has its information from the Central Party Control Commission, which in turn has its information from the District Party Control Commission, which questioned Grabner at a special session in Leuna, neatly noting down the views he expressed ('Ulbricht hasn't got a clue about culture,' 'The party isn't always right,' 'It's fine to listen to West German radio.') and then sent them via Berlin, for the purpose of further processing Grabner, to Leipzig, where they are now slammed down on the table as Master Evidence of his Conservative Worldview (MECW), in seven carbon copies, directly behind the gauntlet waiting for its next throw, while Hasso Grabner sits on the other side of the table with his sabre still drawn ('I occasionally adopt a position on a particular problem that I don't hold at all, just because it's an elegant stance for doing battle'), suddenly becomes aware of the looming evidence pile – and all of a sudden cannot say whether he's the Valiant Little Tailor or a fly to be struck dead with one blow (or one book). ('It would have made more sense if I had received this magnificent tome in advance. I see that other people also have copies.')

What follows is not an answer, but a staccato of questions: 'What's your position on our party's policies?' 'Is what Comrade Walter Ulbricht said to be affirmed or negated?' 'Has the Bitterfeld Path proved fruitful or not?'

And because Grabner says nothing, because he can't say a thing during the chairman's monologue… 'Don't you want to understand these questions, have you not understood them, or don't you want to acknowledge them?'

And that's the moment when it occurs to Hasso Grabner that he's still got his sabre in hand. ('In general, my contradictory spirit is highly developed.') And off he goes. With poems! And why not? After all, the party has summoned Grabner before the commission partly because he recently made trouble at a lyrical evening, inciting a poetic punch-up.

Flashback to the *Leipziger Volkszeitung*, 9 to 30 January 1963. Newspaper documents from a land before our time. The players:

500 audience members, 17 poets, 2 reporters, 1 butcher, 0 literary scholars.

The thing doesn't start with rhyme and metre, though, but with a blunder. When the newspaper ('official publication of the Leipzig Regional Committee of the Socialist Unity Party of Germany') announces the event ('Poets on the Side of the Party'), the culture editor misspells one of the young poets' names, which neither the proof-reader nor anyone else at the newspaper notices, because nobody knows who in the world Volker Brauner is.

Good old Volker Braun* makes no comment and is secretly glad of the extra *er*, while in the Southwest Cultural Centre the first poet takes to the stage, sees 500 pairs of eyes focused on him, and the cameras provided especially by the SED Regional Committee begin to roll. What follows might just as well have happened yesterday. A Berlin rhymer slings verses at the audience like mud, a man from Halle praises life in his city in lines that smell of cabbage soup, and a Syrian poet reports haltingly on the suffering of his fellow countrymen.

Number 17, the last on the stage, however, is a Leipzig lyricist by the name of Richter – and he's a little out of the ordinary. Why, no one can say. Perhaps it's because of the number 17, which traditionally signifies the end of the world and the transition to a new one, but perhaps also because he feels like it, *because he's simply a bit sad that evening*; in any case, the poet from the Pleisse recites a four-liner and declares he's yearning for a womb to take him back, for: 'perhaps we are all born too soon'.

Icy silence in the auditorium. No one applauds. No one, except one man…

It is – who else could it be? – Hasso Grabner who defends the poem before the running cameras of the frozen functionaries, and who, in the subsequent discussion with the audience, also adopts a position against the party, which in turn obviously finds the four-liner anything but edifying:

'The comrade has written a poem marked by resignation, which can only appeal to people who still doubt our development. Can our party approve of it? Poetry has a specific task to fulfil in society.' And to Grabner: 'You're of the opinion this kind of poetry should be offered to exert influence on our youth through their education?'

'First we have to ask ourselves whether poetry exclusively and always has the task of educating,' Grabner responds. And then: 'That this poem has no educational value, that much is clear to me, but in my opinion, it is not teaching anyone to commit suicide.'

'You must bear in mind what authority you have. I sometimes get the impression you're not always aware of the significance of the words you speak.'

'It wasn't me who brought along the poem. All I can say is, nobody's going to die from it.'

'But we can't promote ideas about suicide in today's socialism.'

'I'm just affirming this man's right.'

'But publicly.'

'That won't hurt us.'

'It will hurt us if he still wants to be in his mother's womb in our day and age.'

'There have always been world-weary people, and there still will be in a hundred years' time.'

And so it goes on. And while the party condemns the four-liner and Hasso Grabner never tires of defending the poem and explaining to the functionaries how he sees the matter ('For me, it's a harmless little flower,'), a young man gets to his feet two rows back and claims no one's allowed to say what they want in the GDR, not just on matters of poetry but in general, whereupon Hasso Grabner abandons his poetry analysis, now grown rather boring anyway, and yells, 'Yes, you really can't say the truth!'

What follows is moderate pandemonium, continued in the subsequent days not in the hall but in the *Leipziger Volkszeitung*, and that means in front of not 500 but 500,000 people. With one difference: Hasso Grabner can no longer make a riposte, because after this whole thing he's out on his ear at the newspaper. Firmly ensconced on its pages, however, is the party; it owns the paper. And because the following story would be nothing without a pinch of irony, the Leipzig SED Regional Committee lets the Free German Youth launch the attack on Grabner, the very organisation that Grabner himself founded, 17 years previously.

The usual accusations follow, only this time they're not in his cadre file but in the newspaper. Grabner, it says, is doing nothing less than 'slandering our societal order', by negating 'the leading force of the party of the working class' and is thus 'distanced from the life of our nation'. And because even an FDJ secretary has to say a word or two about poetry when considering a poetry evening: 'Grabner said one ought to give the imagination free rein. That boils down to putting the case for anarchy in artistic creation.'

Two days later, the next FDJ secretary jumps on the bandwagon, followed by a dozen readers concerned about the state of the country's poetry ('Scandal!'), a folklorist ('I only use one measure for the quality of a poem: Is it folkloric?'), and a butcher from the Delicata state-owned production facility ('Being interested in poetry myself...').

That spells the end of Grabner's publishing career, for the time being. Over the coming days, weeks, months and years, none of the pieces he writes for the *Leipziger Volkszeitung* get printed, finished books are no longer published, and poems are cancelled without warning shortly before appearing on the page. The party's cadre department is kept very well informed of all this, meanwhile, and a note on his file remarks, not without satisfaction, that Grabner now only 'earns 60 to 70 marks a month' on average.

The rest, that is, the *political* end of Grabner's career, is dealt with at the sixth Socialist Unity Party Conference in Berlin, held in parallel to the poetry debate, at which the FDJ head condemns both the long-suffering Leipzig lyricist ('Some idiot babbling on about his wish to be taken off the earth. Is he in his right mind?!') and Hasso Grabner for defending him ('It is irrefutably not a question of a minor four-line poem, but of essential issues of worldview and politics.').

Grabner's 'misconduct' is thus noted at the highest level – and that note is not deleted. Files are the raw material of this ideology, trained as it is in obedience to the cadre – and reminding people of those files is an oft-repeated method of demanding greater obedience.

No wonder the party-conference minutes are dug up by the Regional Party Control Commission again, three years after the Leipzig poetry debate, and presented to Hasso Grabner on his summons to interrogation. Unfortunately, though, Grabner has no intention of letting himself be interrogated, instead sitting at the table with his sabre drawn. 'I will no longer stand to be constantly referred to as a shabby rascal on the basis of these completely nonsensical files.'

And then, aimed directly at the commission members: 'Throw the files away, then we won't have any more complications.'

A serious suggestion. Not, however, for the members of the Regional Party Control Commission, who do nothing but dig down deeper into the file in reaction to Grabner's suggestion – and are glad someone has been kind enough, due to the volume of collected misdemeanours, to append a table of contents, including summaries of all his crimes.

Hasso Grabner, meanwhile, is still sitting at the table with his sabre drawn. By now he is more certain than ever that the party has to put up with people like him. And especially with a couple of weltschmerz-y poems. ('We have to tolerate something like that. I myself will only ever write in the artform of Socialist Realism, but I don't consider it dangerous, or a threat to us, when others do not.')

In general, he thinks, it would become the party better if it were to discuss matters with those who think differently, and allow public criticism; that would be a benefit and not harmful. After all, there were almost only bourgeois reactionary newspapers when he was young, in the Weimar Republic, and he, Hasso Grabner, still became a good communist nonetheless, no matter how many penalties the party imposes on him.

And that is the moment in which Hasso Grabner is overcome by the feeling he's been through all this before. Four times, to be precise. They can't put him back on the factory floor now though. And if they do then it cannot be a punishment, because it's what everyone is supposed to do now. And he, Hasso Grabner, has already been there anyway, in Gröditz, Bitterfeld, Stalinstadt, Leuna… This time he won't go though, this time he's staying put, stays seated, leans back, puts his sabre away – and falls silent.

The Regional Party Control Commission has meanwhile read the summary of Hasso Grabner's collected misdemeanours and switched to thinking aloud about his behaviour.

'He overestimates himself.'

'He can't keep his mouth shut, he has to learn to restrain himself.'

'After 1945, not yet mature or ready, he was placed in functions where he never knew how to moderate his own political opinion.'

And to Hasso Grabner:

'We would suggest that you state your position on the facts.'

But Hasso Grabner doesn't state a position; all Hasso Grabner does is stare them down. In the new type of party, he realises all at once, there is no place for the old type of people.

Hasso Grabner could spend some time with that thought. Or write it down. But he doesn't like it. And they won't print anything of his now anyway. Aside from that, it's not a nice thought. Far too fatalistic for someone like him. And even if he did, the Regional Party Control Commission is meeting in the Writers' Association building – that's no place to think about the party, it's a place for thinking about literature!

So Hasso Grabner thinks of a book. A book with a very nice title. It's called *A Farmer and a Farmer's Wife Conceive a Farmer's Son Who Wants to be a Farm Hand**. But the book is not yet printed. It's not even written yet. And once it is written and printed, it won't be by Hasso Grabner. Because 1966 is not 1968. And East Germany is not West Germany. And the men on the other side of the table won't let him go, they just keep talking and talking. About him, the suddenly silent Hasso Grabner.

'... but where do the roots of his ambivalent behaviour lie? What is his real opinion?'

'The views in his poetry, in his official poems, are fine.'

'But then again, he has an ideology here that's not fine at all. Where does this contradiction come from?'

'Hasso didn't become a writer voluntarily; he was stripped of his high-ranking function and he was too arrogant to take on a minor function. He's always written poetry, so he must have said to himself: That's my new job.'

'Hasso merely sells his commodities.'

'He's a manager. He always has to be doing deals.'

'And he's clever enough to know what's in demand.'

'Hasso writes the sort of poems he considers worthless when other people write them.'

'He writes them because they're needed, but I think if he could write like he wanted to, a socialist Rilke* would come out.'

'He said himself his favourite poet is Rilke.'

'He's a split personality.'

'I mean to say, I consider him a hopeless case.'

'He's sitting there with a grin on his face, but we can't take him to task for that.'

And lo and behold, the session ends without a resolution being passed, the seven valiant discussants simply incapable of agreeing what penalty the party should impose on Hasso Grabner this time. ('I'm not in favour of a strict or official reprimand, he'd just laugh at us.' – 'I think relegation is an excellent approach.' – 'Issue a warning!' – 'A warning seems rather insufficient, to me.') One thing they do know for sure though: 'We are in agreement that he must be called to responsibility by the party.' And they take their fat MECW files and get to their feet to go, but they don't get to leave – because that's the moment when Hasso Grabner also stands up, grabs the gauntlet from the table and, with his characteristic sense of the celebratory, addresses a few words to the members of the Regional Party Control Commission: 'Where are you off to? A round of cards? I'll come with you, you arses.'

Yes, you can play a round of cards with the arses from the Regional Party Control Commission, even if they don't want to admit it later on ('Hasso came and joined us!'), thereby driving the chairwoman of the Writers' Association crazy, she having hoped the meeting would reform Grabner's character. ('If I had a four-hour party meeting about my behaviour behind me, I would have gone home and thought about the mistakes I'd made, not gone to the pub.')

Hasso Grabner does go to the pub. He does it because he has known the Unity Party that wants to bring him into line for half an eternity and is aware of the fallibility of each of its members – and because he can read the schizophrenia that rules them all in their very eyes. They're sitting right opposite him, after all, on the other side of the table. And if someone sits opposite you, you can look them right in the eye.

But what about those Hasso Grabner doesn't see? Those that are not on the other side but on his side of the table? Or don't have a face, or wear his own face? What does Hasso Grabner do about them? What *can* he do about them?

Hasso Grabner's Stasi surveillance begins on 12 October 1961. On that day, in Department V/1 of the Ministry for State Security's Leipzig Regional Administration Office, a Stasi lieutenant by the common-or-garden name of Klaus Fischer starts a file that he titles 'Writers' and classifies – in finest East German secret-service style – a 'Pre-emptive Group Operative Process'. In it, he writes: 'The unofficial materials and indications justify the urgent suspicion that the (freelance) writers to be operatively processed – Lindemann*, Bräunig*, Bartsch* and Grabner – take a hostile stance towards our Workers' and Farmers' State, with the main form of their hostile activity consisting of political-ideological diversion.'

Twelve days later, Fischer formulates the surveillance objective in his opening report: 'As the four named individuals are urgently suspected, due to their negative attitude to the party and our Workers' and Farmers' State, of not only acting as agitators but also of sowing political-ideological diversion in the literary field, it is suggested to set up a group operation on them and to process them operatively with the aim of arrest.'

The man chosen to process them operatively is called Heinz Callus, an informal informer to the Stasi and, to judge by his name, a man with thick skin. The fact that the name is a code name is part of the story Lieutenant Fischer plans to write. Callus's task is to check 'whether the individuals named in the operation function as an organised group and possess a joint conception.'

Yet the only thing Grabner, Bräunig, Lindemann and Bartsch have in common is their training at the Leipzig Literature Institute, whereby the quarrelsome quartet's years as students are some years past, mainly between 1955 and 1957, in Grabner's case even by distance learning, as at the time he was 150 kilometres away from Leipzig, busy running the biggest building site in the republic and setting up the Schwarze Pumpe industrial complex, which meant he had just as little time to attend lectures as he did for the regulation internship in a nearby brown-coal plant.

No wonder hard-skinned Heinz has little to show for three months of snooping. His calloused hands have to type an admission to Lieutenant Fischer in his report of 29 January 1962: 'The processing of the individuals accused in the operation has shown to date that these individuals do not constitute a unified hostile grouping.'

A setback, certainly, but that doesn't stop Lieutenant Fischer from continuing the snooping and sleuthing. To keep tough-skinned Heinz on board, though, he is unceremoniously promoted from informal informer to the rank of secret main informer.

And Grabner? While Bräunig takes a lecturer's job at the literature institute, Bartsch and his file move to Berlin and Lindemann is himself recruited as a Stasi informer in May 1962, Grabner is separated from the group operation and granted his own file, courtesy of Lieutenant Fischer. Instead of a 'Writer' he is now called a 'Careerist'.

Not that the Stasi lieutenant knows how to make the state saboteur sing like a canary, and it's clear that one Heinz alone is not enough, especially if you want to play a round of cards with Grabner, because the game requires three people, or better yet, four (someone has to deal the cards), but the arses from the 1962 Regional Party Control Commission are out of the equation, or rather not in the game yet, which means Lieutenant Fischer has to look around for some other arses.

And lo and behold, he finds some. And they're a whole different calibre. Not arses sat flat like the ones from the Regional Party Control Commission. Oh no, what Lieutenant Fischer drags along is round arses, apple arses, in other words, female secret-informer arses!

Now, in the summer of 1962, two at once are put on Hasso Grabner's case. After all, as Lieutenant Fischer notes with a certain satisfaction, Grabner did receive 'a still unacknowledged party penalty for moral degeneracy' in 1952 and is generally 'unrestrained in relation to the opposite sex and to alcohol'. Women clearly make the best wild cards to get the provocative player to show his hand, checking out along the way which cards this cheat named Grabner puts aside face-down.

Except, as always, it turns out differently, and the only person keeping his cards face-down is Lieutenant Fischer, because at the end of the round, in December 1962, he has nothing whatsoever to show against Grabner in his report, which doesn't divert him from his arrest plan, however, but encourages him to put another female operative on Grabner's case to get him to show his hand, 'if necessary supported by the initiation of intimate relations.' In other words: the Queen of Hearts is not playing Old Maid here.

The informal informer, requested especially from Karl-Marx-Stadt to relocate to Leipzig, calls herself 'Wolf' and only dresses herself in sheep's clothing because the Stasi is hungry.

Though this may sound like an irony of history, it isn't one at all, and if it is then it's not the main one, because that's 11 years back…

Back then, in October 1951, the SED heads in Leipzig had openly confronted the steel king (and womaniser) Hasso Grabner with the possibility of being targeted by female agents, warning him to take care. With one difference: at that time, the party feared the agents would come from the West and exploit Grabner's responsiveness to love affairs to get hold of politically charged information. So the cadre craniums had words with him. ('You have an important function. What will the enemy do?') Only that led nowhere in Grabner's case, because he knew what was afoot – and was as sure of himself as ever. ('I know the enemy will try to send a woman agent my way. They haven't done it yet.')

Now, though, 11 years later, the women agents are here, not from Munich or Hamburg but from Leipzig and Karl-Marx-Stadt. But at heart that's only consistent; after all, his 'enemy' has also changed camps and now comes from his own team.

And yet there's one thing that remains unmoved by this historical irony – and that's Hasso Grabner's big mouth. Even under interrogation by his comrades, he can't keep it shut…

'…me becoming dependent on a sexual partner, such a relationship is impossible!'

'Did you know these women that closely?'

'No.'

'What control do you have, if they spend even two days in West Germany or West Berlin?'

'None, but I don't have any control in the GDR either.'

'That's a different matter, in the GDR we have our security organs.'

The security organs. The Stasi. The organ now sending women to hunt Grabner down 11 years later. Because Grabner the fox is not red enough for them. Or the wrong shade of red. In Lieutenant Fischer's eyes, Grabner even tends a little towards the brown of the Nazis, having encapsulated himself from the comrades in Buchenwald and obtained a special position there... But that's not yet enough for the Stasi lieutenant, because he knows this Grabner is a wily fox, he's no easy prey. So the Stasi lieutenant paints him a more lurid shade with his words. If he's brown enough, he thinks, he'll get to keep this Grabner for himself, then the hunt will be over and done with.

And so, Lieutenant Fischer notes in October 1962:

'Grabner enjoys negative discussions in the presence of non-party members. For instance, he negates the inhumane conditions in Buchenwald concentration camp and makes light of events in the 999th penal battalion. In addition, he was promoted to private first class in the penal battalion and was awarded the Iron Cross 2nd class.'

It's the same old game. Some make history and others rewrite it. The communist forced to don the Wehrmacht uniform becomes a soldier decorated by the Nazis, and Buchenwald prisoner number 5334 becomes a Buchenwald denier. In fact, only a few months after the war, Grabner had reported on the cruel conditions in the camp in a brochure published by the Leipzig KPD, and paid a literary tribute to one of his fellow inmates, the pastor and resistance fighter Paul Schneider, tortured by the Nazis and murdered in 1939 with an overdose of strophanthin.

Now, however, in October 1962, no one in the GDR wants to know about resistance-activist pastors, certainly not if it's to do with Buchenwald, where the official party line has it that the barracks were stuffed full of communist heroes who drove out the Nazis of their own accord in April '45, then founded a socialist super-state, then conceived millions of junior antifascist resistance fighters with the aid of their heroically waiting wives and, when the juniors were senior enough, shaped them into a people's army whose combat groups built their own shooting range on the concentration camp grounds, a place of preparation for future acts of heroism...

No wonder no one in the GDR wanted to know anything about any 'homosexuals, gypsies and conscientious objectors' held in Buchenwald.

Now, though, on 23 September 2014, the stories come together in an inconspicuous room in the camp archive, lines both large and small begin to converge, and it becomes clear to me that Grabner only ever told unheroic or even funny stories from Buchenwald because he did not want to be instrumentalised. Anyone who's seen a friend moving barrows full of shit across the light and dark squares of a concentration camp and dying of it won't be a pawn in anyone's game, no matter whether black or white, brown or red, whether it's 1939 or 1962.

But there's another reason for Grabner's behaviour: pragmatists, as I'm only beginning to realise now, are by their very nature not mythologists. So it's only logical that Hasso Grabner finds nothing heroic about having been beaten by the Nazis. Aside from that, he declares in May '65, as he shows a delegation of foreign writers around the camp's grounds, he was 'lucky to end up in a Nazi concentration camp and not in a Soviet prison or gulag.' One thing was clear in Buchenwald at least: the Nazis had beaten the communists and treated them like enemies, and that means badly. How, though, Grabner openly asks himself and his colleagues, must 'those German comrades have felt, to say nothing of the Russians, who were demeaned and killed in Russian prisons and camps by their own people?'

What Grabner is referring to is clear to everyone present: the Buchenwald concentration camp continued to exist after 1945 and was used by the Soviets until 1950 as a special camp for interning tens of thousands of 'enemies' of the emergent Workers' and Farmers' State. Over 7,000 of them died there. The GDR National Memorial Centre's official statements, monuments and commemorative texts, however, contain not a word about it in May '65, when Grabner visits the camp.

And the Stasi? For once, they're not along for the ride in Buchenwald and they have to admit that the information gathered to date is not sufficient to arrest Grabner. So what can Lieutenant Fischer do? Ask the Stasi Regional Administration Office in Karl-Marx-Stadt for fresh arses? Employ a new thick-skinned Heinz? Ban Old Maid?

The person who comes to Lieutenant Fischer's aid is Hasso Grabner himself. Or to be precise: his big mouth. Having declared to his arch-enemy Paul Fröhlich at a Leipzig party conference that literature has always attacked the powerful and that that is still its task in socialism, in December 1965 Grabner is put in the political stocks at the XIth Congress of the SED Party Committee by that very same Paul Fröhlich, and officially declared an unwelcome author.

The other victim of this demolition derby of a party conference is Grabner's fellow writer Werner Bräunig. The self-appointed guardians of socialist morals ram the pair of them off the literary racetrack.

And thus ends the year 1965, and although Hasso Grabner has managed to evade arrest, his Stasi file is by this point so thick that it makes sense to Lieutenant Fischer to make part of the material 'available to the SED Regional Committee for analysis'.

We already know what comes next: Regional Party Control Commission, hours of interrogation, eloquent sabre-rattling, even more eloquent silence. Officially no penalty, unofficially a publication ban. The subsequent game of cards changes nothing. Hasso Grabner, it seems, has played his trumps long ago.

At least politically. In his private life, in contrast, he has found happiness – the young woman he met in the workers' writing circle in Leuna is expecting his baby. It's a boy. Hasso Grabner first became a father 30 years previously. Back then, the house of correction, the concentration camp and the penal division stopped him from seeing his son grow up. His daughter too, born in 1948, had an absent father. This time around, it all looks much better. Until a divorce judge puts in an appearance.

Being still married, Hasso Grabner tries to get a divorce in 1968. But because, according to the party, the GDR boasts 'unalterable measures of ethics and morals, decency and good manners', the presiding judge not only rejects the divorce petition, but also demands that Hasso Grabner puts an end to the 'immoral relationship' with the young woman and goes back to his wife.

But Hasso Grabner doesn't want to go back, Hasso Grabner wants to stay. So he informs the SED regional management that he had 'never found proper contact to my wife and family' after the end of the war and was only at home, if at all, 'as a lodger'.

And to make sure the cadre craniums, gone grey with Leninist anti-lustfulness ('The revolution demands concentration, increase of forces. It cannot tolerate orgiastic conditions.'), also get the point: 'About 10 years ago I met a woman who corresponded to my ideas of a lifetime companion. I spent a long time considering the matter. After four years, I was certain.'

Love, as any fool knows, is the basic material for such a relationship. Socialist ideology, however, as Hasso Grabner's words show, forces him to express himself in this form about love.

And yet it is love that rules Hasso Grabner's life in 1968. Even though it's a strange emotion, love. All around him, people are rehearsing revolt, the students rising up in West Germany and the whole nation of Czechoslovakia protesting. But what can Hasso Grabner do? And above all: what does he do? The Stasi knows the score, as ever:

'In Leipzig, the counter-revolutionary development in Czechoslovakia was given a lively welcome especially by the writers Erich Loest*, Hasso Grabner, Helmut Richter* and Fabian* in private gatherings, where they wished for or demanded it to be transferred to the GDR.'

That transfer never happens and all in all, the revolutions falter. In Czechoslovakia, hope for socialism with a human face ends in the wheel arches of Soviet tanks, while in West Germany the students' conscious revolution and the writers' and artists' dreamed uprising produce a heap of shards, albeit not in the mirrored palace of capitalism but in the glass house of their own camp, and the only thing left for Hasso Grabner at the end of this *annus mirabilis* of 1968 is love – and literature.

The Cell, his autobiographically tinted novel about a communist resistance group in a Leipzig engineering factory during the Nazi era, is published in a print run of 10,000 copies. This time the party has no objections. According to an assessment report, the book is 'clearly awareness-raising and partisan'. But that's not enough. That same year, in autumn '68, two new editions of Grabner's 1966 world-war novel *Classified: Norsk Hydro* are issued, which will be translated into Polish, Bulgarian and Czech over the coming year and reprinted a number of times.

To add to this grotesque, drifting repeatedly into the realms of schizophrenia, the majority of Grabner's books are brought out by Deutscher Militärverlag, the official publication arm of the GDR's National People's Army. When Grabner starts writing, his short stories find a home there, because they deal with his time in the penal battalion and fit into the catalogue. When he can no longer publish as a result of his criticism of the SED in 1965, it is his direct line to the publisher that saves him. The two of them were in the Waldheim house of correction together 30 years before – and a connection like that lasts a lifetime.

In 1967, the military publishing house brings out Grabner's *Reckoning with the Devil* in a print run of 125,000 copies. Now, though, in the winter of 1968, the devil does his reckoning with him – and this time Hasso Grabner can't do a thing about it.

Hasso Grabner, the writer, has left Leipzig and moved into a tumbledown house with his new family deep in darkest Brandenburg, on an island in a river. The locals call the house the 'Jew's Palace', as it was built in 1925 by the Jewish architect David Seiden, who later perished in Theresienstadt. Seiden's client was the Jewish lawyer Richard Rosendorff, but he was forced to leave the house in 1934, whereupon – what strange mirror image – a writer moved in with his young wife and two small children. He didn't stay long either, though. After the pogrom of November 1938, the house was left a ruin, destroyed by Nazis in the false belief that it was still owned by a Jew. When Hasso Grabner moves in 35 years later, the bathroom tiles are still cracked from the stones thrown at them.

The island in the river is a place of tacit agreements. From the day on which the locals first catch sight of the new arrivals, they are convinced that the almost 60-year-old man of the house must be a well-paid writer and that the young woman by his side is only after his money. But Hasso Grabner is broke. And the young woman by his side is expecting no money, only a second child.

In other words: the situation is happily crap, and the books Grabner works on unceasingly in the rotting, damp house may have large print runs, but they don't bring in much money, or at least not enough to pay off the pile of debts from all the years of slim pickings.

But that's how it is: normally a man with a straightforward, guileless face, a roguish joker, in 1968 Hasso Grabner spots schizophrenia in the mirror, reads the hypocrisy that rules them all in his own eyes one morning.

And so it is that in December '68, Hasso Grabner, the proponent of revolution who once propagated the GDR take up the same course as Czechoslovakia, writes three handsomely paid comment pieces for Radio Vltava*, the very propaganda broadcaster that condemns the Prague Spring and justifies the invasion of Czechoslovakia by Warsaw Pact troops. With the money he gets, Hasso Grabner pays off debts. His personal slate, he knows, can't be wiped clean this way. Anyone who makes a reckoning with the devil always has an outstanding debt in the end.

Hasso Grabner is now 57. He has abandoned the idea that his generation has the task of redeeming the world. The only place where that idea is still to be found is in his early poems. It has been 10 years since they were published. Ten years turned by history into an eternity. Certainly no sign of redemption in sight. The end of history is squatting beneath the horizon, laughing its head off. His own end, meanwhile, comes ever closer.

Hasso Grabner's face has grown thin. And his hair grey. And his heart, on the left, is already beating a stumbling rhythm. High time to marry the young woman by his side.

But the divorce judge still refuses, so Hasso Grabner has to wait another two years. Then his wife dies. He was married to her for 38 years but he rarely saw her. First it was the house of correction, the concentration camp and the penal battalion that kept them apart, then it was his work, and in the end, it was love. To finish off, time severs the connection he could not.

When Hasso Grabner spontaneously strides to the local registrar while on a family holiday in Bad Saarow in December 1972, and declares he wants to get married the next day, he knows he doesn't have much longer to live. What he doesn't know, though, is that in the GDR you can't just get married from one day to the next. And certainly not if you're planning to do it away from home. But what is Hasso Grabner supposed to do? Everyone in the place where he lives thinks he's already married. And he has no time. At least not the four weeks that the registrar insists upon. But because Hasso Grabner is as stubborn as a mule, and the registrar wants to get rid of the old man and the young woman he has brought along to testify to and corroborate his wish, she grants the odd couple the possibility of a 'socialist marriage'. Nuptials of this type, she explains, can be arranged within the space of 10 days, but require the presence of a production collective, a speech by a production-brigade head, and permission from the local SED committee.

In other words: there's no way out of the situation. Then again, has there ever been a way out? Back in the Albanian mountains? As an assistant bookseller promoted to steel king of an entire occupied zone? As a brown-coal prince? As a poet with nine books sold?

Hasso Grabner gets to work immediately.
The local party committee has no objection.
The young woman by his side brushes all health concerns aside.

The moment Grabner has the local committee's permission, he writes a letter to friends in a nearby steelworks and asks to borrow their collective for his wedding. One of his friends having since been promoted to director general and – of course – been in Buchenwald with Hasso Grabner, he not only sends the requested collective, but comes along himself. There isn't a brigade head with them, but they hire an actor to hold the requisite socialist speech. Faced with the odd-looking wedding party, the actor promptly gets cold feet, so Hasso Grabner plays the Buchenwald card and asks the director general to hold a speech ('We've been through much tougher times than this, don't let me down now.'). Any old speech will do.

And the director general speaks. About Hasso Grabner, the restless stormer and stresser, the man who, always accompanied by the party, has a long path of socialist development behind him, now to come to its crowning socialist conclusion in the form of a socialist marriage.

Seeing as everyone but the registrar knows what kind of show is going on here, the ceremony soon turns into a divine comedy, its only truly socialist act the signing of the marriage certificate contained in a folder red as a flag.

Now Hasso Grabner might actually die in peace. As the doctors see it, he ought to, in fact. But Hasso Grabner doesn't consider it for a moment. Hasso Grabner, the pragmatist with the tendency for cheerful schizophrenia, prefers to go to an alternative practitioner. After a while, he decides that the man – with his views, methods and devices – is a relic of an irrational, unscientific and hugely unenlightened time, and is reminded of his old communist education addiction as the pendulum sways to and fro above him; he gives a gentle smile, not knowing what about, is prescribed a few droplets – and returns to health.

Or at least to sufficient health to start writing again. Back in 1969, he had won the GDR Ministry of Culture's award for young-people's books, absolutely unexpectedly, for his novel *Anka and Big Bear*, and in the same year the Theodor Fontane Prize for Art and Literature. Then in 1970 he revised and abridged his novel *The Cell*, in 1971 wrote *The Ship in the Dark* and then sat straight down to work on his *Macedonian Duel*, which is published in 1973. But the writing desk is never enough for the eternally restless Hasso Grabner – so he flies to Bangladesh in February 1974.

He has received an invitation from the Bangladeshi writers' association. But the GDR authorities know a man like Hasso Grabner will do as he likes even in the poorest corner of Asia, and they refuse him an exit visa. Unable to find any other author willing to represent the country in Bangladesh (and because Grabner's wife is a scholar of Asian studies), however, they end up granting his application.

The feared fuss doesn't come about. At least not until the last day of the trip, when Grabner is slated to give a reading at the GDR embassy in Dhaka. The previous day, the Russian writer Alexander Solzhenitsyn* was expelled from the Soviet Union for the publication of his *Gulag Archipelago*; the East German ambassador feels obliged to justify his Russian friends' actions and asks Grabner for a statement as well. He ought to have known better...

Barely has Grabner been granted the floor, when he declares that he generally refuses to believe verdicts that refer to individuals as scum, enemies of the development of socialism and agents of imperialism, not only because he, a convinced communist, has himself received a number of party sanctions, but also because he, just like Solzhenitsyn, was interned in a camp himself, and it is not his place to doubt what such a man has written.

Silence in the room. No one dares to say a word. Even the ambassador is struck dumb.

Back in the GDR, Grabner continues where he left off in Bangladesh in the local branch of the Writers' Association, whereupon first the SED functionary in charge of writers and then the chairman of the Association of Victims of Nazi Persecution turn up at the house on the island. Grabner is not at home, so the functionaries warn his wife that her husband can no longer rest on the laurels of his resistance-fighter past – it will no longer protect him.

Shortly after that, in the autumn of 1974, Grabner travels to West Germany to visit a friend. On his return, he is stopped at the border and subjected to a full body search, while the car he is in is taken apart. It takes six hours for the customs officers to find what they're looking for: books by Hannah Arendt*, Rosa Luxemburg* – and Solzhenitsyn's *Gulag Archipelago*.

For the border guards, it's a clear-cut case of importing imperialist reading matter. But Hasso Grabner protests. Against the slurs against these writers. Against the regulations on what he is allowed to read and what not. And against the books not being returned to a man like him, who spent years in a house of correction and a concentration camp under the real imperialists. He will be contacting the Politburo in person to get his books back!

But Hasso Grabner doesn't get his books back. What Hasso Grabner gets – of course – is an invitation to the Regional Party Control Commission.

He might as well get out his pack of cards already. But Hasso Grabner doesn't live in Leipzig any more, he lives in the no man's land of Brandenburg – and there's no one to play cards with here. What they do have is the usual arses. And yet one thing is different now; the quality of the interrogation has shifted over the years. The members of the Regional Party Control Commission, as Hasso Grabner sees at first glance, are all a generation younger than him.

It is October '74. The GDR is now 25 years old. A quarter of a century as a republic. A blink of an eye for a realm. And yet time enough to eliminate the old communists who were born in the Weimar Republic and had grown into the movement through anti-Nazi resistance, time enough to get rid of their generation. A demographic demobilisation or social selection, it doesn't matter which. Those who held protective hands over Grabner for so long now have nothing more to say – and will never do it again. Even Fritz Selbmann, the friend, the cellmate, the heavy industries minister, the man who used a bulldozer to break the ground at Schwarze Pumpe and was so big and powerful that his arm stretched from Leipzig to Dresden and back again, even Fritz Selbmann is on his deathbed.

The only ineradicable (and eternally rejuvenating) things are the institutions. The Regional Party Control Commission demands self-criticism from Hasso Grabner in December '74. But Grabner considers the possession of works by Luxemburg, Solzhenitsyn and others worthy of anything but criticism and continues to insist on the return of his books, so he is struck from the list of comrades of particular merit in the resistance against the Nazi regime, and the party does not invite him to its commemorations of the defeat of fascism on 8 May 1975.

Grabner, however, is happy to go without the three pounds of smoked eel that each of the still officially meritorious resistance fighters is given there. Their cost, he says, is 30 pieces of silver per portion – and he has already made his reckoning with the devil.

The reckoning with the party is yet to come, however, for the institutions are not only ineradicable and eternally rejuvenating, they also never forget, and in February '76 Hasso Grabner is presented with the next summons to the Regional Party Control Commission.

But that's how it is. History doesn't repeat itself; it just doesn't like changing its outfit. Prefers never to get undressed at all. Its muse, Clio, I think to myself, simply leaves her clothes on. Black dresses. Red dresses. White dresses. Dresses for mourning. Dresses for comedy. Dresses for the purity of the Epigoni.

February '76, in any case, is like the same month 20 years earlier. Snowstorms. Plunging temperatures. Russian winter. Siberian shock. Everything grinds to a halt in Brandenburg's no man's land. The only thing still running is the Schwarze Pumpe industrial complex. Hasso Grabner, meanwhile, lies still in his bed. He is trapped there by pneumonia, and his slowly dying heart muscle adds to the agony.

By the time he appears before the Regional Party Control Commission in March, there is no way out of the situation. But then, there never was. Yet he, Hasso Grabner, has managed it every time. And even received honours, medals and awards. Now, though, his journey comes to an end with the pen-pushers of the Regional Party Control Commission. There's no prize to win here, and the only chance for Hasso Grabner to escape this room and its four walls of imitation wood panelling is to put his own life in the balance.

Hasso Grabner starts right away. Hasso Grabner lays his whole bizarre life bare – and ends up in a bare-knuckle battle with the Regional Party Control Commission. And why not? Confrontations with the party are part of life, after all, and not for nothing has Hasso Grabner brought along a quote by Rosa Luxemburg about freedom of the press, of choice and of speech, a quote which ceremoniously declares that a state proscribing what its citizens may read, say and think is not a dictatorship of the proletariat, but a dictatorship of its political leaders.

What follows is one last drama.

Never, yells the Regional Party Control Commission chairman, will he tolerate such accusations. Never will shoddy and shabby imperialist literature flood the GDR. And never did Rosa Luxemburg say such a thing.

Hasso Grabner could demand his confiscated book right now and look up the relevant passage. Or – like back in Leipzig – simply sit there in silence. But Hasso Grabner prefers to get out his sabre one last time, swipe the gauntlet from the table with its tip and declare that he was risking his life when the esteemed Regional Party Control Commission chairman was still in short trousers, risking it for the communist cause, and so the esteemed Regional Party Control Commission chairman has neither the right to tell him what and what not to do, nor the authority to throw him out of the party.

There is no time left, that much he knows, for further words. So he opens the door behind him, steps out of the room and leaves.

In the Gaps of the Record Lies Happiness

The way out of the book
is the way into the book.

1

I am not sure, but I think this might be how to begin. With an afterword that is really a back story. A little digging for lost traces at the end of the book. A detective story to round it all off. The tale of the hidden start to the story.

Yes, that might be the best place to start, although I don't want to pretend I went looking for Hasso Grabner. How could I? I hadn't read a single one of his books. I knew nothing about him. I didn't even know a man named Hasso Grabner existed.

What I actually wanted to write was a book about forgotten writers, writers who had once been acknowledged, but then somehow fell between the cogs and sprockets of time and came out again forgotten. Or rather, never actually came out again. And if they did, then in a million pieces.

That's how I imagined it, at least: a book of stories about writers nobody remembers, a kind of telephone directory for the no longer reachable. A book of munching and mulching, composed by time itself and narrated by me.

That was what it was going to be – and it started just fine. By the time I came across Hasso Grabner, I had already found three suitable candidates. A Czech poet put into an asylum and forgotten there. An English poet who got lost in his own home. And a South African poet of whom no one could say whether he'd been black or white.

That wasn't bad to begin with, but a glance at my selection told me that if I carried on like this, I might rescue a few poets from oblivion but I could forget about sales figures for my book. One thing was for sure: I wasn't going to make my fortune with a crazy Czech, a reclusive Englishman and an unspecified South African. If people in other countries forget their own poets, that's fair enough (or bad enough), but it's better (that is, worse, and thereby better after all) if they have been forgotten in their own country – and are remembered there then again.

But having been forgotten was only one of the criteria I wanted to meet; I didn't want to write a book about poets plagued by page indentations, publishers and prepositions. I wanted to write about writers who had experienced something, gone into battle against the great cogs and sprockets of time. Not only with the pen in their hand, but with weapons of all kinds. Rogue elephants, not just paper tigers! Feat-starters, not just seat-farters! Life, not just lyrics!

The only problem was: which German writer met those criteria? And which of those who met them had been forgotten? And most importantly: how do you find a forgotten writer?

The fact that I only asked myself that question once I'd found the first three was to do with my not having looked for them. I had stumbled across them by chance, and it was my good fortune that they'd been shunted onto the very same siding. It was quite easy, in fact. The Czech knew the Englishman, the Englishman knew the South African, and when I cried 'Hooray!' upon reading that the South African had been forgotten even during his own lifetime, the other two raised their heads.

Now it was different, though, because I had a plan, or a desperate wish, to link my readers to my book via their shared country. Except unfortunately, I had shunted myself onto the sidings. How was I to find a forgotten writer when I had no idea who had been forgotten? I wasn't a literary historian (and I'm still not.). I had no idea about poets (and I still don't.). When it came to poetry collections, I've read precisely zero over the past 20 years – and before that only one, to make sure I didn't fail my German exam.

That meant the route to choosing the poets couldn't be: I know this poet, he or she has been forgotten. It had to be: he or she has been forgotten, I have to get to know them.

But how does someone who doesn't read poetry find out about forgotten poets? Especially about poets who not only struggled with metre, but also took on life's full magnificence and malevolence?

2

If you don't make progress by yourself, you have to start with others.

I admit that logic is rather dubious, especially for someone hoping to make it as a (literary) detective, but those were the facts. And a detective who doesn't stick to the facts won't solve a single case. Not even his own. And lo and behold, once I'd accepted that, it was no longer all that difficult to come up with a suitable search strategy; in a time when secondary outnumbers primary literature, and even the most obscure run-of-the-mill poet has their own Wikipedia entry, there could only be two criteria for those who were forgotten: *no* secondary literature and *no* Wikipedia entry.

Thus, the parameters were defined, and all I needed now was a list of writers, to find one among them who had been destroyed in the faithful struggle against the world's adversities and then forgotten, along with his oeuvre. So the next day, I went to my nearest city library, planted myself in front of the shelf labelled 'German Literature', took a deep breath – and grabbed the first reference work I came across.

It was the *Encyclopaedia of German-Language Writers. From the Beginnings to the Present Day*, compiled by the state-owned Leipzig Bibliographical Institute and published in 1974. The revised edition, that is. The first version of the book dates back to 1968, and that edition was based on an encyclopaedia from 1960, which also had a predecessor…

To cut a long story short, the list was not exactly brand new, and the majority of the listed writers are presumably dead by now, but seeing as I was looking for forgotten authors, that was more of an advantage than a disadvantage. In other words: I could now get going. Not from the beginning but from the middle, as the book I had picked was volume two of the encyclopaedia, letters L to Z. When I opened up the pages I found a card stuck in the front noting the previous borrowing dates. The most recent stamp was from 23 January 1978. It looked like I was on the right road.

I was soon typing the first writer's name into a search engine. My goal was clear: as soon as I didn't find anything on a writer, I'd start researching him or her. And the list helped me. It was a wanted list, and I hoped that at least one entry would be a dead end. Probably, though, there would be lots of dead ends, probably the encyclopaedia was full of forgotten writers, and then I'd have to choose one. But that would be step two. Step one was to use this old book from a defunct state to find a forgotten poet, shipwrecked in the great sea of literature, to whose paper island no one had yet built a bridge.

Except there wasn't one. Someone else had already written something about every poet, and someone had provided secondary literature on all the essayists, novelists, critics and children's book writers listed in the encyclopaedia; even the radio and television writers were taken. They had even devoted a book to writers who did literary adaptations.

No matter who I looked up, I found further literature about them – here a book, there an essay, there a website. And those that weren't listed anywhere at least had a Wikipedia entry.

It was wonderful and at the same time sad. None of them had been forgotten; time had provided each one of them with their personal biographer. Whole armies of authors had set out in search over the years, and all of them had found their little king, had built him a pedestal of footnotes beneath the paper island and set up a throne of text on top of it.

By the time I came along, all the land had been grabbed, and I saw that there was nothing more to be had; the others had got there before me…

The day ended as it had begun – in front of the shelf labelled 'German Literature', except that this time I didn't take a book off the shelf, I put the encyclopaedia back.

It was essentially an act of self-assurance, a disclosure of my own actions to myself, the final confirmation of what I had done all day.

I had spent 11 hours looking for a gap in the record, failed to find one, and now I was demonstrating my defeat to myself by closing the gap in the rows of books.

Once that was done, I decided to cheer myself up by checking on the Wikipedia homepage who had died over the past few days.

I've been doing that for years. It's a kind of ritual, and maybe one day I'll write a story about a man who spends his days reading death notices of writers – not because he wants to commemorate them, but because he wants to make money out of them. And with good reason. The man runs an antiquarian bookshop, but business has been bad for some time, and his only chance of survival is to put books by freshly deceased writers in the window – and whack the price up as he does. The man knows that death is the point when people remember a person, death is the point when they start to get sentimental – and there's nothing better for making money than sentimental people.

On that day, however – it was 19 September 2013 – no writer had died, and the only people who had bitten the dust, according to Wikipedia, were a Japanese businessman, an American footballer, a Polish philanthropist, and a Canadian porn actress.

Googling the porn actress seemed a little impious under the circumstances, and only owning a video store on the brink of bankruptcy could have changed that. But first of all, I didn't own a video-hire business, secondly I was in a public library, and thirdly I wasn't trying to make money out of remembering, but out of forgetting. I did at least recall at that moment why I was there and that I was trying to write a book about lost writers – and that it had been a pretty stupid idea to get so carried away by the prospect of selling 10 more books as to start looking for someone who had got lost here in Germany. At least if it meant spending 11 hours digging deep into an old encyclopaedia and still not finding anything in the end.

That is, I had found something after all, but not in the old encyclopaedia, in the new one, right next to the column of recent deaths. Under the heading 'On this day' for 19 September, there was a list of all kinds of battles, births and bills of law. Which also informed me that that day, 19 September, was International Speak Like a Pirate Day.

By the time I left the library there wasn't much left of Pirate Day. And even if there had been, it wouldn't have changed the bind I was in. I was a buccaneer on an ocean of paper. I was sailing in search of a ghost ship to plunder. I was trying to bail water with a colander.

3

The next day, of course, all was forgotten. I was back in the library, back in the German-literature section, back at the shelf. There were all manner of encyclopaedias there; I would just get myself a new one and find something useful – and that's what I did.

This encyclopaedia bore the name *GDR Science Fiction: Authors and Works*, was published in 1988 and – as the GDR had itself become an object of that kind of retrospective science fiction generally known as history writing – represented the largest possible overview that could possibly exist on the subject. And this was where I found my forgotten writer.

The article on him and his work was short, there was no further literature available on him, and the fact that he did have a Wikipedia entry was not all that bad. Firstly, the entry was only 10 lines long (practically non-existent); secondly, I had set my selection criteria on a purely theoretical basis, without fully understanding the state of the material (and thus felt forced to change them now that I knew how idiotic they were in practice); and thirdly, it was a Friday (which needs no further elucidation).

In short: I had him. Here was the man I'd been looking for. And he also seemed to have led an exciting life, or at least the small amount of information I found about him made it look like he'd had all sorts of adventures: born in the place where the Nazis had built the V2, postwar childhood, apprenticeship in the socialist Workers' and Farmers' State, varied artistic interests, contact to Joseph Beuys in Düsseldorf, trouble with the East German Ministry of Culture in Berlin, banned from writing, fled to West Germany and started over in a town famous for people whipping each other with stinging nettles during the annual marksmen's festival…

That sounded like exactly the mix of comedy and drama I'd been looking for. And there was enough writerly material too; this man whose name I had never heard before had left a substantial body of work: novels, poetry collections, children's books, as well as graphic art, illustrations and even a dissertation on top.

The fact that he'd only lived to 50 fitted the image I had of him – a picture of an exciting life, a life just waiting to be told.

I wrote to the publishing house that had brought out his books.
But nobody wrote back.
I tried to get in touch with his family.
But nobody answered.
I asked a number of archives if they knew anything about him.
But they said they'd never heard of him.
After three weeks' work I had nothing to show for it.
It seemed I had found the forgottenest of the forgotten writers.
I didn't feel like starting a new search.

The encyclopaedia could go take a flying leap.
I gave up.

4

In series one, episode five of *Little Britain*, wheelchair user Andy Pipkin is pushed around his local library by his friend Lou Todd. Lou asks whether Andy has seen any books he'd like to borrow. But Andy doesn't look at the books. He doesn't care what's on the shelves. All he does is stare straight ahead, point to the right and say, without the slightest idea of what he's actually pointing at: 'I want that one.'

It's a book about Chinese history.

Lou tries to persuade Andy against it and offers to take a different one. Andy agrees, points at another book without looking and says: 'I want that one.'

It's a book about the origin of the Chinese language.

Lou tries again. And Andy also does his best. Asked which book he'd like, he once again points blindly to his right and says: 'That one.'

It's a second copy of the book about Chinese history.

Lou gives up. Andy now has three books. I, on the other hand, had spent three weeks pointlessly trying to find a forgotten writer, found two encyclopaedias in which I first found everything and then nothing, and finally – thanks to my television consumption – came across an idea.

5

On 7 October I was back at the library, planted myself back in front of the shelf labelled 'German Literature', closed my eyes, took a few steps, stopped somewhere, stretched out my hand and said 'I want that one.'

When I opened my eyes, I was holding a small book from the Reclam publishing house. It was a greasy paperback, very well thumbed. The cover was ripped and the spine only held the pages together with the aid of sticky tape. It looked like plenty of people had already picked up this particular book, and something told me that wasn't a good sign for finding a forgotten writer.

The book was called *GDR Portraits*, although the letters 'GDR' were covered over by the library sticker, as though trying to visually express the country's disappearance. The shelf number was 74-8-15711, with the first number standing for the year of publication – which meant the book had come out in the same year as the encyclopaedia, another sign that wasn't exactly a good omen.

The reason I still didn't put the book straight back on the shelf was that it was almost 600 pages long. So many, I thought, that they might have forgotten just one.

But forgetting is one of those things. And the book was certainly one too. Firstly, hardly any of the 50 portraits was of writers, and secondly, these individuals had already been immortalised by these portraits, which meant my only chance to find a forgotten writer in the book was to look not at the people portrayed, but at those who had *written* their portraits, and to hope that one of them had slipped beneath the radar of subsequent generations.

So that was what I did. Copied the name of the portrait writer out of the book, entered the name of the portrait writer in the search engine, and if there was nothing there then off to the library catalogue, to a specialist database, to the Deep Web, as far and as deep as I could get, always in the hope of coming up against a void, a gap, a forgotten writer – a completely insane procedure, driven by a search for nothing and fed by the names on a table of contents held together with adhesive tape: Walther Victor, Jan Koplowitz, Peter Nell, Maximilian Scheer, Paul Wiens, Erwin Strittmatter, Dieter Noll, Max Schroeder, Louis Fürnberg, Anna Seghers, Stephan Hermlin, Günter Kunert, Olaf Badstübner, Stefan Heym, Bernhard Seeger, Bodo Uhse, Franz Fühmann, Barbara and Werner Bräunig, Ernst Schumacher, Hasso Grabner – Bingo!

Or in fact, not bingo at all. Not a single hit. Nothing but a newspaper article that began with the words: 'What a life story. It is both astounding and regrettable that it has never been documented…'

What followed was a report on an event marking the centenary of Hasso Grabner's birth, coupled with a brief outline of that life story: born in 1911, bookseller, communist, prisoner in Buchenwald, Wehrmacht soldier in a penal battalion, after the war director general of the entire East German steel industry, then works director of the gigantic Schwarze Pumpe industrial complex, in between demoted over and over by the SED, countless party sanctions, and yet every time he got back on his feet and grabbed life by the collars with pragmatic jollity, later a writing career, numerous novels and poetry collections, his work now largely forgotten – a bizarre life, a crazy biography…

Except: why in the world had nobody written about this Hasso Grabner before? And why had not even Wikipedia heard of him? How could a man with a life story like this have been forgotten?

6

Once the detective has found his forgotten man, his first task is to reconstruct the unknown life. His second and far more difficult task, however, is to find reasons why he was forgotten in the first place.

To put it succinctly: I don't know why Hasso Grabner came to be forgotten. But I do know that he vanished all over again when I set out in search for him.

In the books about the places where Hasso Grabner spent parts of his life, there is barely any mention of him. In most, his name is not even named, and even where he does put in an appearance, he is only ever a marginal figure, a footnote in the game of history, another minor character standing on the edge of events and looking down into the great gulf of the century.

While I was searching through books and articles for Hasso Grabner, there were times when I felt as though the few facts I knew about him were nothing but fiction, as though Hasso Grabner's life were a mere invention and none of it had really happened. It was as though he had never been in the Waldheim house of correction, had never worked in the library at Buchenwald, as though the German invasion of Greece had taken place without him. And yet he was there, in all those places, and when I think about it now, it's as though what had taken place in the Buchenwald library as a stroke of fortune had repeated itself after Grabner's death in these libraries and archives as a stroke of *mis*fortune.

Hasso Grabner was too small to be noticed, and too big to be only ever washed along by history. He was a second-class hero, a man not in the front row and thus of no interest for those who decide over life or death, remembrance or oblivion – the historians and the executioners.

For them, Hasso Grabner was not even third choice, so they first let him live and then forgot him, and it took a minor anniversary ceremony for anyone to notice that his life offered first-class material for a story.

But even if the reason for Hasso Grabner's disappearance was a different one – what counts is that I found him. With the aid of a reporter who gave me a hint of his amazing life. With the aid of Hasso Grabner's wife, who invited me into her home so she could tell me about her husband. And with the aid of a thick sheaf of files that someone plucked from the depths of an archive and handed over to me with the words that I wasn't actually allowed to read what was inside them.

But that's how it is, isn't it? Once the detective runs out of probabilities, coincidence comes to his aid. And a few well-meaning people. And then – then all he has to do is fit the pieces together. And at some point, a few steps further along, this book begins…

Acknowledgements

Writing a book about Hasso Grabner meant above all tracking down lost trails and, once I had finally discovered them, learning to read them. In this case, I needed not only countless books, files and other sources, but also and importantly a number of people who helped me to locate, view and put together the jigsaw pieces found in all sorts of conceivable and sometimes inconceivable places. I owe many heartfelt thanks to:

Sigrid Grabner – who let me into Hasso Grabner's life
Sabine Stein – for her support of my research in Buchenwald
Sylvia Ehl – for the documentation of Grabner's time in the concentration camp
Sascha Lange – for the notes on Grabner's work as a young communist
Hans-Peter Klausch – for his information on the 999th penal division
Doris Ullrich – for her research on Hasso Grabner in Corfu
Jim Potts – for the photos and documents on wartime Corfu
Hans Herwig Brunner – for his research on the Neunkirchen reserve field hospital
Rüdiger Bernhardt – for information on the Workers' Writing Circle in Leuna
Sonja Berthold – for the pictures and information on Grabner's time at VEB Montan
Gerald Kolditz – for finding Grabner's files in the Saxon State Archive in Leipzig

Selected Bibliography

The following list contains all the works cited directly in the book, as well as a selection of books that helped me to understand the context of Hasso Grabner's wondrous life story.

Setting Out

Sigrid Grabner: *Jahrgang '42. Mein Leben zwischen den Zeiten*, **Leipzig 2003**

No One Knows Any More

Frauke Gränitz (ed.): *Daten und Fakten zur Leipziger Stadtgeschichte*, Leipzig 2013

Sascha Lange: *Meuten – Broadway-Cliquen – Junge Garde. Leipziger Jugendgruppen im Dritten Reich*, Cologne 2010

The City behind the Walls

Martin Habicht: *Haftbedingungen und antifaschistischer Kampf im Zuchthaus Waldheim 1933–1945*, East Berlin 1988

Karl May: *Mein Leben und Streben* (reprint), Hildesheim 1997

Hainer Plaul: *'"Besserung durch Individualisierung". Über Karl Mays Aufenthalt im Arbeitshaus zu Zwickau von Juni 1865 bis November 1868,'* in: *Jahrbuch der Karl-May-Gesellschaft* 1975, pp. 127–199

Weimar

Hasso Grabner: *'In memoriam Pfarrer Schneider,'* in: Kommunistische Partei Deutschlands, Stadt und Kreis Leipzig (ed.): *Das war Buchenwald! Ein Tatsachenbericht*, Leipzig 1945, pp. 89–94

Lutz Niethammer (ed.): *Der 'gesäuberte' Antifaschismus. Die SED und die roten Kapos von Buchenwald*, Berlin 1994

Torsten Seela: *Bücher und Bibliotheken in nationalsozialistischen Konzentrationslagern. Das gedruckte Wort im antifaschistischen Widerstand der Häftlinge*, Berlin 1992

Karl Heinrich Stein: *Tilman Riemenschneider im deutschen Bauernkrieg. Geschichte einer geistigen Haltung*, Vienna 1936

Leaving
Hans Burkhardt, Günter Erxleben & Kurt Nettball: *Die mit dem blauen Schein. Über den antifaschistischen Widerstand in der 999er Formationen der faschistischen deutschen Wehrmacht (1942–1945)*, East Berlin 1986

Hans-Peter Klausch: *Die 999er. Von der Brigade 'Z' zur Afrika-Division 999. Die Bewährungsbataillone und ihr Anteil am antifaschistischen Widerstand*, Frankfurt am Main 1986

Greek History – An Outline
Hagen Fleischer: *Im Schatten der Kreuzmächte. Griechenland 1941–1944* (2 volumes), Frankfurt am Main 1986

Gert Fricke: *'Das Unternehmen des XXII. Gebirgsarmeekorps gegen die Inseln Kefalonia und Korfu im Rahmen des Falles "Achse" (September 1943)'*, in: *Militärgeschichtliche Mitteilungen* 1/1967, pp. 31–58

Hasso Grabner: *Der Streit um die Partisanen*, East Berlin 1958

Christoph Schminck-Gustavus: *Kephallonia 1943–2003. Auf den Spuren eines Kriegsverbrechens*. Bremen 2004

Gerhard Schreiber: *Die italienischen Militärinternierten im deutschen Machtbereich 1943 bis 1945*, Munich 1990

Heading Home
Hermann Frank Meyer: *Blutiges Edelweiß. Die 1. Gebirgs-Division im Zweiten Weltkrieg*, Berlin 2008

Intermezzo – Leipzig, April '45
Jürgen Möller: *Die letzte Schlacht, Leipzig 1945*, Bad Langensalza 2014

Gerhard Steinecke: *Drei Tage im April, Kriegsende in Leipzig*, Leipzig 2005

At Home
Günter Bayerl (ed.): *Braunkohleveredelung im Niederlausitzer Revier. 50 Jahre Schwarze Pumpe*, Münster 2009

Arnolt Bronnen: *Deutschland. Kein Wintermärchen. Eine Entdeckungsfahrt durch die Deutsche Demokratische Republik*, East Berlin 1956

Spelling It Out
Heinz Czechowski: *Die Pole der Erinnerung. Autobiographie*, Düsseldorf 2006

Hasso Grabner: *Die Zelle*, Halle (Saale) 1968

Ideologische Kommission der SED (ed.): *Protokoll der von der Ideologischen Kommission beim Politbüro des ZK der SED und dem Ministerium für Kultur im Kulturpalast des Elektrochemischen Kombinats Bitterfeld abgehaltenen Konferenz*, East Berlin, 1959/1964

Klubleitung VEB Leuna-Werke 'Walter Ulbricht' (ed.): *Neues Lied, das da beginnt …*, Wittenberg 1960

Thomas Reichel: *'Sozialistisch arbeiten, lernen und leben'. Die Brigadebewegung in der DDR (1959–1989)*, Cologne 2011

VEB Leuna-Werke 'Walter Ulbricht' (ed.): *Neues Lied, das da beginnt. Brigadetagebuch. Versuch einer fotografisch-literarischen Neugestaltung mit Arbeiten des 'Zirkels schreibender Arbeiter' des VEB Leuna-Werke 'Walter Ulbricht'*, Leipzig 1963

Wolf Wondratschek: *Ein Bauer zeugt mit einer Bäuerin einen Bauernjungen, der unbedingt Knecht werden will*, Munich 1970

Translator's Glossary

999th penal battalion
Beginning in 1942, the 999th penal division conscripted those men previously pronounced unworthy of defending Germany, mainly ex-prisoners. About a third of them had been sentenced for anti-Nazi activities, and took the opportunity to defect to the Red Army in droves or join resistance groups in Greece and Yugoslavia. Although some 37,000 men passed through the various battalions, by its dissolution on 1 May 1945 the division consisted of only five soldiers.

A Farmer and a Farmer's Wife…
The second book by the West German writer Wolf Wondratschek, a poet, who also wrote prose. First published in 1970 under the title *Ein Bauer zeugt mit einer Bäuerin einen Bauernjungen, der unbedingt Knecht werden will.* The book calls attention to the class structure of the West German left around 1968 – where the sons of the bourgeoisie clamoured to join the working class.

Apitz, Bruno
Communist writer and founding member of the → Socialist Unity Party. He was not particularly prolific, perhaps because his function in the East German Writers' Association kept him busy. His key work, the 1958 novel *Naked Among Wolves*, was set in Buchenwald concentration camp and translated into 30 languages. The English version (tr. Edith Anderson) was published by Seven Seas, a Berlin-based publisher of English-language books – what a bizarre idea.

Arendt, Hannah
German-American political theorist and historian. Having compared Stalinism to Nazism in her 1951 *Origins of Totalitarianism*, she was not in the → SED's good books.

Bartsch, Kurt
Critical East German writer, moved to the West in 1980 after publishing a poetry and prose collection entitled *Cadre File*.

Braun, Volker
I once sat behind Volker Braun at a reading and couldn't concentrate because I'd read one of his books as part of my degree and was overcome with awe. He worked as a builder at → Schwarze Pumpe before studying philosophy in Leipzig and writing his first poems. Probably best known as a playwright, he is still revered as one of the → GDR's great critical writers.

Bräunig, Werner
Excellent East German writer, author of *Fairground* (tr. Samuel Willcocks), an unfinished novel about a village with a uranium mine, a paper mill and of course a fairground.

Communist Party of Germany (KPD)
Existing from 1918 to 1933 before being banned and hounded by the Nazis, the party had its headquarters around the corner from where I live in Berlin, now named → Rosa Luxemburg Square, although it's triangular. During Hasso Grabner's time it was the largest communist party in Europe, led by → Ernst Thälmann.

Derbyshire, Katy
Translator and publisher of this book, writer of these notes.

Fabian
The author and I don't know who was being referred to here, and would prefer not to speculate.

Free Democratic Youth (FDJ)
Initiated in exile, the Free Democratic Youth was the only state-recognised youth organisation in the → Soviet Occupation Zone

and the → GDR. Tasked with raising responsible socialists, it became almost inescapable for 14- to 25-year-olds and officially organised youth culture across the country, running clubs and holiday camps and staging the annual Festival of Political Song from 1970 to 1990. The FDJ still exists, on a homeopathic scale.

German Democratic Republic (GDR)
From 1949 to 1990, the fifteen districts in the eastern chunk of Germany constituted the German Democratic Republic. Its capital was East Berlin, while a wall was built around capitalist West Berlin in 1961 to stop mass emigration from the east. The GDR called itself a 'Workers' and Farmers' State' and was ruled by the → Socialist Unity Party, which practiced 'actual existing socialism', a pragmatic compromise worthy of Hasso Grabner, an impromptu dictatorial picnic on the untrodden path to communism.

Kapo
Kapos were concentration-camp prisoners with special privileges who supervised their fellow inmates, an early form of outsourcing used both to cut SS personnel costs and to divide and conquer. What the kapos did with their power was largely up to them – from librarian recruitment to murder.

KPD
See **Communist Party of Germany**

Kuntz, Albert
Coppersmith and communist Albert Kuntz became a → KPD MP in 1932, only to be put into "protective custody" by the Nazis in 1933. He was murdered at Mittelbau-Dora concentration camp, where he had been organising the sabotage of the V2 missiles built in underground chambers by prisoners and forced labourers. A nearby football stadium is named after him.

Lindemann, Werner
East German poet who later wrote children's books, father of Rammstein's singer.

Loest, Erich
East German writer and journalist for the *Leipziger Volkszeitung*. Left the Writers' Association in protest against censorship of his work and emigrated to West Germany in 1981.

Luxemburg, Rosa
Founding member of the → KPD, murdered by right-wing freikorps guards in January 1919. Despite accusing her of excessive spontaneity and leaving her more radical works unpublished into the 1970s, the → SED made much of the anniversary of Luxemburg's killing, holding annual demonstrations on that date. As you might imagine, her belief that a country's freedom is determined by just how free dissenters are was not appreciated in the → GDR and played an important role among dissidents.

May, Karl
Conman, petty criminal and extremely successful adventure novelist. One of Germany's most-translated writers of all time, his biggest coup may have been to instil his readers with a deep love of his entirely imaginary Wild West. East Germans in particular still revere his native American character Winnetou, along with the screen adaptations filmed mainly in 1960s Yugoslavia – another pragmatic solution worthy of Hasso Grabner.

National Committee Free Germany (NKFD)
Originally formed by German soldiers in Soviet POW camps and communist exiles in the Soviet Union, the NKFD published a weekly newspaper and numerous political flyers. It also broadcast messages from vans along the Eastern Front, aiming to persuade members of the Wehrmacht to defect or surrender.

Nenik, Francis
Francis Nenik is a pseudonym.

Radio Vltava
Fake Czech radio station produced from East Berlin between August 1968 and February 1969 in an attempt to combat the Prague Spring. The announcers spoke accented Czech and Slovak, and the content was plainly propagandistic, spreading conspiracy theories and false information, discrediting Czechoslovakian reformers and media. Listeners soon realised what was going on and protested, spelling the end of the station.

Richter, Helmut
Prolific East German writer, poet and lyricist. Wrote the lyrics to the 1978 pop hit 'Über sieben Brücken musst du gehn', covered by Chris de Burgh as 'Seven Bridges' in 2011.

Rilke, Rainer Maria
Dead white man, German poet. Liked big cats.

Schwarze Pumpe
Originally the name of a village, the Black Pump Gas Combine was built partly by Hasso Grabner and eventually consisted of several interconnected gas works, briquette factories, coking plants and power stations. It also had its own residential areas and infrastructure, including a medical clinic and a central kitchen. Unlike its builder Hasso Grabner, the industrial complex was awarded the Karl Marx medal in 1977.

Seifert, Willi
After leaving Waldheim and Buchenwald, Seifert climbed the → GDR career ladder. He was second in command on becoming deputy chief of police during the 1953 uprising, when the Soviet Union intervened, and again in 1961, as deputy minister

of the interior, when the Berlin Wall was built. They made him a lieutenant general a year later. Unlike Hasso Grabner, he was awarded eight different East German medals.

Socialist Unity Party (SED)
Established in April 1946 by forcibly fusing the Communist and Social Democratic Parties, the Socialist Unity Party of Germany united only the communists and social democrats in the eastern chunk of Germany, the → Soviet Occupied Zone that became the → German Democratic Republic (GDR). And only those who didn't object to being united with their former foes. I had a boyfriend once whose grandfather allegedly refused to be in the same party as those dirty social democrats.

Soviet Occupation Zone
As agreed between Roosevelt, Stalin and Churchill at the Yalta Conference, the Soviet Union occupied the eastern chunk of Germany from May 1945 until the foundation of the → German Democratic Republic in October 1949.

Solzhenitsyn, Aleksandr
Critical Russian writer, Nobel laureate in 1970. After writing about his experiences of life in a gulag, he was expelled from the Soviet Union and flown out to West Germany in 1974. → GDR officials considered him morally corrupt. My father, also bearded and cheerful-looking but considerably younger, was once mistaken for Solzhenitsyn by a British television presenter, while working as an assistant sound recordist.

Thälmann, Ernst
Former ship's stoker and name-giver to a characteristic peaked cap, Stalinist head of the → KPD from 1925 to 1933. He also led the Red Front Fighters Alliance and founded Antifascist Action. The Nazis arrested Thälmann as soon as they could and left

him to rot in various prisons for 11 years, then murdered him in Buchenwald concentration camp in August 1944.

Ulbricht, Walter
A Leipzig-born comrade of → Ernst Thälmann in the pre-Nazi-era → KPD, Ulbricht co-founded the → NKFD before returning from his Moscow exile unscathed in 1945 and in 1950 became chairman of the → SED's Central Committee, making him the most powerful man in the → GDR. (I do like these arrows.) He was ousted in 1971 by Erich Honecker, who doesn't get an arrow because he's not mentioned in this book.

Untermensch
A term ('under man') coined by the American eugenicist Lothrop Stoddard and enthusiastically adopted by the Nazis, usually rendered back into English as sub-human. I have chosen not to translate it, because I despise the notion behind it and would like it to remain a historical term.

Volkssturm
Another move to recruit as many men as possible, the Volkssturm was formed in September 1944 and consisted of 16- to 60-year-olds without standard uniforms, sworn to loyalty to Hitler and equipped with substandard weapons. After years of indoctrination, many defended their towns vehemently, particularly as the Red Army advanced from the East. Untold thousands of them died fighting as the Nazis scarpered.